ALLEN IVERSON

FEAR NO ONE

JOHN N. SMALLWOOD JR.

POCKET BOOKS

New York   London   Toronto   Sydney   Singapore

The sale of this book without its cover is unauthorized. If you purchased this book without a cover, you should be aware that it was reported to the publisher as "unsold and destroyed." Neither the author nor the publisher has received payment for the sale of this "stripped book."

An *Original* Publication of POCKET BOOKS

 POCKET BOOKS, a division of Simon & Schuster, Inc.
1230 Avenue of the Americas, New York, NY 10020

Copyright © 2001 by John Smallwood

All rights reserved, including the right to reproduce this book or portions thereof in any form whatsoever. For information address Pocket Books, 1230 Avenue of the Americas, New York, NY 10020

ISBN: 0-7434-4590-2

First Pocket Books printing October 2001

10 9 8 7 6 5 4 3

POCKET BOOKS and colophon are registered trademarks of Simon & Schuster, Inc.

For information regarding special discounts for bulk purchases, please contact Simon & Schuster Special Sales at 1-800-456-6798 or business@simonandschuster.com

Front cover photo by Allsports

Printed in the U.S.A.

This book is dedicated to my niece, Teale Simpson, and my nephews, Ian Candelaria and Brayden Simpson.

"Remember, when you dream, you can achieve anything."

Love,
Uncle Johnny

Contents

CONTENTS

A L L E N
IVERSON

FEAR NO ONE

Introduction

What makes an athlete compelling? What makes an athlete interesting? Controversial?

For some it is because of their extraordinary talent, skills, and athleticism. For others it is because of their flamboyant personalities, intriguing history, or cutting-edge style.

But rare is the athlete whose story contains all of these characteristics.

Philadelphia 76ers superstar guard Allen Iverson may not be the most controversial athlete of the last decade, but he is certainly one of them. Although he only entered the National Basketball Association in 1996, he has been in the national spotlight since he was sixteen years old. From his arrest as a high school All-America to his years at Georgetown University to becoming the first overall pick in an NBA Draft to his Most Valuable Player season, Allen Iverson's life has been a rags-to-riches story like few others.

He has become a symbol of the dichotomy of sports in America, equally praised and criticized for his independence, brashness, flare, and ability. To a society in cultural and generational flux, he represents both the deepest fears and the brightest hopes.

"I've said it a million times, there are going to be a billion people who love Allen Iverson and a billion people who hate him," Allen has said. "I don't know why some people dislike me. I play basketball. I take care of things off the court. Why criticize me when I'm trying my hardest?"

His is the story of both the upsides and downsides of life as a famous celebrity. It is also the American Dream, but it's one that many are afraid to embrace because it comes with all of the rough edges that we so often like to pretend do not exist.

Allen Iverson grew up in extreme poverty, living in a neighborhood plagued by drugs and violence, a place that squashed more dreams than it allowed to escape. But it was this climate that forged his dogged determination to make a better life for himself and his family—and it shaped his ability to view the world in a clear, straightforward manner.

"I wanna be the best basketball player that's ever played the game," Allen says. "Number one, because I think I worked that hard to be that. And number two, this is my profession, and I wanna be the best at what I do.

"I know that when I leave the game, some people will still say he is not the best player that ever played the game. But I know in my mind that I will have tried to be."

In the 2000–2001 season, the twenty-six-year-old Allen Iverson took a giant step in that direction.

From his summer of discontent in 2000, where he was

almost traded, Allen raised his level of play and carried the Sixers to their greatest season in nearly two decades. Along the way he became an All-Star, the league's leading scorer, and the shortest MVP in NBA history. He brought his team within a whisker of winning the world championship.

He silenced critics while still staying true to himself.

At the beginning of the season he was still being mentioned as the poster child for everything that was wrong with modern professional sports, and by the end of it, he was being hailed as the brightest new face of the NBA.

The truth has always been in between. He's been under intense scrutiny since he was a high school junior, navigating the trials and errors of adulthood in the biggest fishbowl imaginable. Consequently, it seems his every action is automatically placed in the plus or minus column of his growth, maturation, or worthiness of being called a role model.

"I'm still the same person," Allen says. "I'm just older, wiser. I've never changed who I was. Philly is everything to me. I always wanted to be a Sixer. I wanted to be the first pick (in the draft).

"I almost left here. I had to get better as a player, but first I had to get better as a person. I had to listen a little better.

"(The Sixers) were talking about getting rid of me. I heard a lot of negative things, even from some fans. I just kept working. Eventually they accepted me for who I was inside, not my hair, my jewelry, who I hang with, my music."

The path to greatness is often paved by the lessons learned from the past. As Allen Iverson moves forward, his

NBA career now seems headed down a road that could eventually rank with some of the greatest of all time.

His journey has not been easy, and at times he's paid a heavy price for the mistakes he made along the way. But in the end, his is a story of persistence, a reminder to all that questions don't have to be an unpassable obstacle as long as you keep looking for "THE ANSWER."

1 Born into Poverty

This was different for Allen Iverson. He was the 1996–97 NBA Rookie of the Year. He was named Most Valuable Player of the 2001 NBA All-Star Game. He had just been named league MVP for the 2000–2001 season.

But this was the NBA Finals—Iverson's first ever and the Philadelphia 76ers' first since 1983.

As always, all eyes would be on Iverson. And all that stood between him and the ultimate reward for a season of remarkable growth, acceptance, and recognition were Shaquille O'Neal, Kobe Bryant, and the defending champion Los Angeles Lakers.

The Sixers were the largest underdogs in NBA history. The question wasn't if the Lakers would beat them, but just how many games would it take.

Typically, Iverson was not fazed.

"Pressure?" Iverson asked before Game 1 of the NBA Finals. "This isn't pressure. This is basketball. This is fun. This is what I love to do. Pressure is coming from where I come from. And growing up the way I had to grow up. That's pressure. That's life."

Ann Iverson was fifteen years old when she found out she was pregnant. She had just made the girls basketball team at Bethel High School, and after taking her physical, she was told she was going to have a baby.

Having grown up in the ghettos of Hartford, Connecticut, Ann, the oldest of four siblings, had just relocated to Hampton, Virginia, to live with her maternal grandmother. Ann's own mother had died at the age of thirty, after becoming ill due to complications from a previous medical procedure.

"When my mother died, I remember running outside in the rain and shouting, 'What kind of God are you to do this?' " said Ann, who was twelve at the time. " 'How could you do this?' "

Ann knew who the father of her unborn child was. His name was Allen Broughton, and the two had gone to grade school together in Hartford. He had said he loved her and would be there for her.

Like many young men who are suddenly faced with the awesome responsibilities of fatherhood, Broughton may not have fully understood everything that meant.

"My intentions were to move down to (Hampton)," Broughton once told *The Philadelphia Daily News*, "but I was only fifteen years old. Then she got involved with someone, and I got involved with someone. We never had a chance to be together."

Ann Iverson was still a child herself, single, frightened, stuck in poverty, jobless, and about to become a mother.

Into this world came Allen Iverson, born on June 7, 1975, in Hampton.

"What is it—a boy or a girl?" Ann Iverson recalled asking on the day Allen was born.

She remembered that friends had told her to pray for a boy, so that she would have someone she could count on to help her through the difficult times that were ahead of her.

"Thank you, Jesus," Ann Iverson said when she was told she had a son. "I remember I was so amazed—this was a real baby. Not a baby doll, but someone I would have to care for. I remember when I stretched him out on the bed to check him out, his hands came down to his kneecaps. I got so excited.

"I thought, this little boy is going to play ball!"

Shortly after Allen was born, Ann Iverson brought him to Hartford to meet Allen Broughton, but as she looked around the neighborhood, she decided that this was not the place she wanted to raise a child.

"I looked around at these people hanging out, the drugs being sold," Ann said of the neighborhood where she grew up. "I told myself, 'No way am I ever coming back here.' "

As a consequence, Allen Broughton was out of Ann and Allen Iverson's life by the time the baby boy had turned three.

Ann Iverson's grandmother had also passed away leaving Ann alone with a son to raise. By the time she was seventeen, Ann Iverson and her son Allen had moved in with her boyfriend, Michael Freeman. Although not his biological parent, Freeman was the man Allen Iverson grew up to consider his father.

"I understand the kind of life we were brought up in,"

Ann Iverson has said of her relationship with Broughton. "I have never, ever blamed him. I have told Allen not to blame him.

"I feel sorry for (Broughton). Not only did he never contribute, he never even called to see how Allen was doing. Allen would look at him today like just another guy he would pass on the street."

Much of who Allen is can be traced back to his relationship with his mother Ann. There's is an uncompromised love, an unbreakable bond.

"She is the person I have always looked up to," said Allen, who has a tattoo of Ann's initials over his heart. "I've never had a sports figure as a role model. It was always her.

"By her always telling me I could do something with my life, I believed her. She used to tell me I could be anything I wanted to be. Some moms in her position would have given up, but she did what it took. I feel I was raised well. I would not have wanted to be raised by anyone else or anyplace else."

Life in Hampton was as tough as it comes.

The Stewart Garden Apartments in the East End of Newport News, Virginia, were a desolate and hopeless place.

The drugs, violence, and prostitution that Ann Iverson had hoped to keep her son away from in Hartford were unfortunately there in the Stewart Garden Apartments as well. Allen Iverson grew up in a world were drug deals and shootings could happen in the middle of the day.

When she was eighteen, Ann Iverson received $3,818 as

part of a settlement from the hospital over her mother's death. But that didn't last long.

Soon she had to deal with a sick daughter. Ann had two daughters with Freeman—Brandy, who was born in 1979, and Iiesha, born in 1991. The medical problems of Iiesha, who suffered frequent seizures, would later play an influential role in Allen Iverson making the biggest decision of his life—to enter the NBA Draft in 1996.

In addition to Iiesha's problems, money was tight. Ann worked at Langley Air Force Base as a secretary, then at New Hampton, Inc. driving a forklift, and then at a local shipyard as a welder.

"She did whatever she had to do to make money to raise her children," Allen Iverson said of his mother.

The home that Allen Iverson grew up in often went without running water and electricity because of unpaid bills. Worse than anything, however, was the fact that a sewage pipe ran right underneath it. Whenever a pipe would burst, and they often did, raw sewage would seep into the home where Allen and his family lived.

"Coming home, no lights, no food, sometimes no water," Allen Iverson said of his difficult upbringing. "Then when there was water, no hot water.

"Living in a house where the sewer was busted and having to watch my sisters walk around in their shoes and socks all day because the floor was wet from the sewage. The smell by itself was making my sisters sick."

Michael Freeman worked in the Newport News shipyards, but a car accident in January of 1988 cost him his job. His family was suffering, and he couldn't find work.

In the end, Freeman was desperate to help his family. He had been in and out of jail for most of his life, so it wasn't that difficult for him to convince himself that committing a crime was not so bad if it was to support his family.

In 1991 Freeman was caught and convicted of drug possession with the intent to distribute.

"I didn't buy Cadillacs and diamond rings," Freeman once said, explaining his illegal activities. "I was paying bills."

Freeman served twenty-two months in prison and then was sentenced to another twenty-three months for violating his parole.

At the time, Allen Iverson said he was mad at Michael Freeman for going to jail, but as he got older, he changed his mind about the man who had taught him to play basketball and took him to pickup games.

"He was just trying to feed his family," Allen said of Freeman. "He never robbed nobody. It would kill him to come home from jail and see how his family was living.

"One time he came home and just sat down and cried."

Allen Iverson was fifteen years old. He hadn't entered the ninth grade. His biological father had abandoned him, and the man whom he considered his father was in prison. His family was poor and living in atrocious conditions. And he was the man of the house.

"When you're the oldest man in the house," Allen said once in an interview, "and your mother is motherless and not much older than some of your friends, and your sister is shaking, and you don't know why you're living in a dark, freezing sewer hole, it occurs to you that there is a lot riding on you."

Life outside of the house wasn't much easier for Allen. Growing up in poverty has its own rules, some that mainstream society doesn't always understand. Allen saw things that no child should have to see, much less live through day to day. His friends and acquaintances were the people he grew up with in his neighborhood. Some of them dealt drugs. Some of them committed crimes. Some of them were in gangs.

And even though Allen avoided the temptation of getting heavily involved in some of the trouble his friends did, they were still his friends. Maybe that was because all of them, including Allen, knew they were living in a harsh situation where sometimes the greatest accomplishment was simply waking up alive the next day.

Over the course of one summer Allen lost eight friends to violent deaths, including his best friend, Tony Clark, who had always been there to stand up for Allen when trouble appeared.

Ann Iverson recalled a conversation she had with her then teenage son. "Ma, I can't be poor. I just can't be poor," she said he told her.

Allen Iverson had a plan to get out of the poverty he had grown up in, a plan that would take him and his family away from all of the hardship they had known.

His plan was basketball.

"I knew I had to succeed for my family," Allen once said in an interview. "People would say, man, that's a million-to-one shot to make it to the NBA, but I'd say, 'Not for me it ain't.' 'Cause if I didn't succeed, well, I don't wanna think about it.

"I thought, for all the suffering they've done. They need me to make it. They ought to have some satisfaction in life.

"I had a bigger picture for my life. I wasn't going to go back to the sewer."

2 | A Star Begins to Rise

Ann Iverson always loved basketball. Her son, Allen, did not.

"I remember the first time I sent (Allen) out to play basketball," Ann Iverson said. "He was about nine. He didn't want to go. He started crying because I made him."

Allen's preferred sport was football. It was more rugged, a tougher game for a tough guy.

"I think I was like nine or ten years old," Allen said of when he first started playing basketball. "But I never wanted to play, seriously. I always thought basketball was soft.

"My mom bought me some Jordans (basketball shoes). I came home, and she was like, 'Here are your shoes. You're going to basketball practice today.' And I was like, 'I ain't playing no basketball. It's soft. I don't want to play no basketball. I don't like basketball.'

"I was crying all the way out the door, and she's pushing me out. I got there and I saw all these kids who were also on

13

my football team playing basketball. I came home and I thanked my mom. I've been playing basketball ever since.

"But I miss football. I never expected to play basketball in the NBA at first. I always felt it was going to be football."

Some athletes take time to find their game, and some know it right away. Despite his small frame, Allen took to basketball immediately. And people began to notice.

Allen said he first started playing ball at Anderson Park in Newport News, Virginia, and then his home court became Aberdine Elementary School in Hampton, Virginia.

"That's where I watched my uncles and my uncles' friends play," Allen said. "They were the people I thought were so nice, so cold on the court.

" I had to play right after school. It was blazing hot, like 105 or something. My uncles and their friends would come to the court at five or six o'clock when the sun was going down, and they ran."

A young Allen wanted to run with them, but at that time they wouldn't let him.

"I guess they thought I wasn't good enough, or I was too young."

That all changed by the time Allen hit the ninth grade. By then, the rumors around Virginia's Tidewater Area were about a basketball prodigy who could dribble as fast as others could run and was virtually unstoppable when he was determined to score.

By the time he reached the ninth grade, everyone knew who Allen Iverson was.

"Then everybody wanted to pick me for their team," Allen said. "They wanted to pick me first. 'Yo, I got A.I.'

"It was just a great feeling because that was where I always wanted to play. Before they were hollering at me to get off the court because I was trying to play while they were playing. Then to go back and be able to play against them and kill them."

Iverson took his game off the street tops and into the gym at Bethel High—the same school his mother was playing basketball at when she first discovered she was pregnant. At Bethel, Allen became a two-sport star in football and basketball, appearing on the varsity football team as a freshman and playing wide receiver and safety.

As a sophomore quarterback/safety in 1991, Allen led Bethel to an undefeated regular season and its first outright Peninsula District football title in fifteen years. He produced 1,583 yards of total offense and intercepted 13 passes.

"I wonder sometimes," Allen's high school football coach Dennis Kozlowski said, "if he would have stuck with football, I think he would have been a major Division I quarterback in college. And after that, who knows?"

"As much as Allen has accomplished on the basketball court, he's not even playing his best sport," said Gary Moore, whom Allen lived with during part of his high school years and now works as Allen's personal assistant. "His best sport is football, and I'm not the only one who will tell you that."

But there were no doubts about Allen's prospects as a basketball player.

During the summer of 1991, Allen exploded onto the college basketball scene when his uncanny scoring led the

Boo Williams AAU team, which was comprised of Hampton Roads All-Stars, to the semifinals of the seventeen-and-under AAU National Tournament.

"Allen had this dream to become a professional basketball player," said Michael Bailey, Allen's coach at Bethel High. "When the first man walked on the moon, that meant Allen could play in the NBA. To me, any dream is a possible dream. He and his mom visualized (his making the NBA) years ago. It would have been crazy for me to say something special wasn't going to happen for him."

Basketball coaches from schools like Duke, Kentucky, and Notre Dame began calling the local newspaper for stories about Allen's basketball exploits.

When Allen missed the second day of preseason football practice in 1992, it was thought that he might have given up football to concentrate solely on basketball. Allen hadn't given up football, and the 1992–93 school year would turn out to be the greatest of his young life.

In the opening game of the 1992 football season, Allen did not start at quarterback for Bethel. But at halftime Coach Kozlowski put him back behind center, and Allen led the Bruins on two scoring drives in their first four possessions as the Bruins won their season opener 21–0.

With Allen leading the way, Bethel reached Virginia's Group AAA Division 5 playoffs. In a semifinal game Allen helped the Bruins rally from a 16–0 deficit to defeat Huguenot High 22–16 and advance to the championship game. Allen capped the comeback by scoring the winning touchdown on a 2-yard sneak in overtime.

In the Division 5 State Championship Game against

E. C. Glass High School, Allen passed for two touchdowns, intercepted two passes and scored two touchdowns as the Bruins won 27–0.

"State football," Iverson said in April 2001 after the Sixers had finally beaten the Indiana Pacers in the first round of the NBA playoffs. "That's the last time I felt this happy. State football, not basketball. How many years ago was that? It was ninety-two. It's been from that whole time for me."

Allen accounted for 2,204 yards of total offense his junior year at Bethel High. He scored 21 touchdowns, passed for 14 more, and had eight interceptions. He still holds the Virginia high school record with five interceptions in a single game.

Allen was named the Virginia Group AAA Football Player of the Year. He was first-team All-State as a defensive back and kick returner and received consideration as the All-State quarterback.

Division I coaches from schools like Florida State, North Carolina, Maryland, and Virginia Tech were recruiting Allen as a quarterback and safety.

"I would look at NFL games and see things Deion Sanders did and know that Allen did them for us," Coach Kozlowski said. "And the thing was we'd get him the first day of practice, and then he would be gone right after our last game, gone to play basketball."

Basketball was still Allen's true calling.

Three days and just one practice after leading Bethel to the state football championship, Allen played the first game of his junior season in basketball and scored 37 to lead the Bruins to a 73–68 victory over Kecoughtan High.

It was the beginning of an amazing season in which

Allen would average 31.6 points, 8.7 rebounds, and 9.2 assists a game. The 948 points he scored broke the twenty-year-old single-season record established by Petersburg High's Moses Malone—Malone, who had gone directly from high school to professional basketball and eventually became one of the 50 Greatest Players in NBA history.

"I knew what Allen could do in basketball," Coach Bailey said, "but there wasn't time to appreciate it. There was always the next practice, the next game, the next thing to do."

But as great as things were going for Allen on the football field or the basketball court, things were getting worse away from them.

Ann Iverson was doing all she could to support her family, but with her boyfriend, Michael Freeman, in jail for selling drugs, their financial situation became desperate. Allen's attendance in school suffered, too, as he would regularly stay home to care for Iiesha. Coach Bailey would often drive by the Iverson home in the morning to pick up Allen to make sure he would go to school. Sometimes the coach would have to travel to several addresses to find him.

"More than once I found out that Allen hadn't spent the night at home because he didn't approve of what was going on there," Coach Bailey once said. "After one of those times, I remember Allen saying to me, 'This isn't the way it's supposed to be, but it's the way it is.'"

Coaches, teachers, and people in the neighborhood would often give Allen money just to make sure that he could eat.

Despite the hardships, there were moments of kindness

too. And some of those people who helped Allen when he was growing up were the same people critics have said he should have abandoned when he became an NBA star.

"My friends made me," Allen would later say. "They're the ones who had something to do with keeping me alive on the streets before I made it to the NBA.

"These are the guys who were with me since day one. These are the guys I trust. And believe me, where I'm at right now, it's hard to trust people, but these guys I trust. If I were to die, I feel real good that these would be the guys who would take care of my family. I know they're going to be straight for me forever. That's the only thing that matters."

Coach Bailey was one of the first people to come into Allen's life that he trusted. His wife, Janet, was one of Allen's English teachers and tutors at Bethel High.

"The smartest thing I could ever do in my relationship with Allen was coach him through my heart," Coach Bailey said. "I could never outmaneuver him, outthink him.

"The only way was through the heart because of the passion he has for what he does. I had to go to him on a level where he would accept me. One thing you learn about Allen is that the people who stand up to him, who tell him what they think, are the ones he respects the most. With Allen, you see the style, but what you get is the substance. And you fall in love with the substance. He is a loving person. You get back as much as you give."

When Allen was named Most Valuable Player of the 2000–2001 NBA season, he made sure that Coach Bailey and Mrs. Bailey had a seat with his Philadelphia 76er coaches and teammates for the awards ceremony in Philadelphia.

"When we had to have our talks, after practice or whatever," Coach Bailey said of his and Allen's relationship at Bethel High, "our favorite place to go was Hardee's.

"I thought about that when Allen made it big time. After one of Allen's summer celebrity games, he said he wanted to take me out to eat. He said, 'I want to go to Hardee's.' Allen doesn't forget anything.

"We'd talk about a lot of things, and one day I asked Allen what he wanted from me. He said, 'Sir, can I say one thing? Always be there for me.' That was all he wanted."

Soon that was going to be what seventeen-year-old Allen Iverson would need from everyone who cared anything about him because his world was about to turn upside down.

It was Valentine's Day 1993. Later in the week Bethel High would play arch rival Hampton on the last day of the basketball regular season.

With issues at home and pressure from playing basketball, Allen was tense. He needed to relax, have some fun, just be a kid for a change, so Allen and some friends ended up at the Circle Lanes bowling alley.

"I sent him to the bowling alley that night," Coach Bailey remembered. "I told him to go do high school things, to enjoy it, to have a good time."

It was to be a piece of advice that would have dire and life-altering consequences for Allen.

3 | Trouble Finds Him

Because he grew up under difficult circumstances, Allen Iverson was always one small stumble away from a calamity. But even though he hung out with a tough crowd, Allen avoided getting into any serious trouble. That is, until he went to the Circle Lanes bowling alley.

Nobody has ever been able to say for sure what exactly happened on the night of February 14, 1993, but the incident would wind up changing Allen's life forever. Until that night, Allen was celebrated in Virginia's Tidewater Area as a superior athlete who was using his gifts to find a way out of the poverty he was born into.

Early that school year as a quarterback/safety/kick-returner, Allen had led Bethel High to Virginia's Class AAA Division 5 Football Championship. And now, as an All-America point guard, Allen had led Bethel to its first Peninsula District basketball title in fifteen years and had the Bruins headed for a run at the state basketball title.

What most witnesses agree on is that seventeen-year-old

Allen and three friends, who were all African-American, were at the Circle Lanes in Hampton, a place where local kids of all races hung out. At some point a confrontation between a group of white kids and Allen and his friends occurred, and an argument ensued. Racial insults were allegedly hurled and soon a physical fight broke out, a fight that eventually involved as many as fifty people and in which chairs were ultimately used as weapons.

On February 16, two days after the fight, Allen led Bethel past arch rival Hampton 69–67 in front of eight thousand fans at the Hampton Coliseum. The victory gave the Bruins their first Peninsula District championship and assured them a spot in the state Group AAA tournament.

At almost the same time not that far away, Hampton police announced that they were investigating a chair-throwing brawl at the Circle Lanes that resulted in three people being sent to an emergency room. Police said they did not know what had started the fight, but four bystanders who were injured by thrown chairs claimed that several high-school-aged African-American males participated in the brawl.

A week after the bowling alley incident, Allen, who averaged 31.1 points, 10 assists, and 11 rebounds, was named to the *Parade* magazine high school All-America first team.

But Allen's happiness was shattered two days later. On Tuesday, February 23, Allen was one of two juveniles arrested in connection with the fight at the Circle Lanes.

Despite his arrest, Bethel High officials decided that Allen would still be allowed to play with the basketball team during the playoffs. That night in the Peninsula District Tournament semifinals, Allen scored 42 points to lead Bethel past Ferguson High 81–78.

While the police investigation of him continued, Allen performed spectacularly. Bethel beat Maury High, which featured 1995 NBA No. 1 overall draft pick Joe Smith, 52–50, to earn the school's first ever trip to the Group AAA tournament quarterfinals.

In the state semifinals Bethel rallied from a 17-point deficit in the third quarter to beat Woodbridge High 72–65 in overtime. Allen's 3-point shot with 26 seconds left in regulation sent the game into overtime.

The Bruins (27-3) would play for their first ever state championship in basketball.

Exactly 14 weeks after leading Bethel to the Virginia Group AAA football championship, Allen did the same in basketball. He and backcourt partner Tony Rutland combined for 58 points as the Bruins defeated John Marshall High 77–71 at University Hall on the campus of the University of Virginia.

With the glory of the basketball season done, however, the attention of the Hampton community started to focus on the case being built against Allen.

A videotape of the fight did not show Allen, and he would later testify that he left the Circle Lanes as soon as the fight started. During the melee, twenty-three-year-old Barbara Steele was hit in the head with a chair, knocked unconscious, and received a gash that required six stitches. Ms. Steele testified that she did not know who hit her, but two other witnesses identified Allen as the culprit—something he denied.

"For me to be in a bowling alley where everybody in the whole place knows who I am and to be crackin' people upside the head with chairs and think nothin's gonna happen to me? That's crazy," Allen would later say in denying the charges.

"And what kind of man would I be to hit a girl in the head with a chair? I wish at least they'd say I hit some man."

The case was to become a controversial issue that divided the town of 130,000 along racial lines.

"People tell me that the only time when things were more tense racially (in the Hampton Roads area) was after the Reverend Dr. Martin Luther King was assassinated," commented David Teel, a sports columnist for the *Daily Press* newspaper, who covered Allen's high school career.

Much of the controversy came from the fact that although as many as fifty people were involved in the brawl and nobody knew for sure who or how it started, only four African-Americans—including Allen—were arrested.

"It's strange enough that police waded through a huge mob of fighting people and came out with only blacks and the one black that everybody knew," Golden Finks, a crisis coordinator for the National Association for the Advancement of Colored People (NAACP), said of Allen's arrest.

Further fueling the tension in the community was the crime that Allen and the other defendants were charged with by the Commonwealth of Virginia. Most, considering the murky circumstances of the fight, had assumed that Allen would be charged with a simple misdemeanor assault and would be given probation. Instead, prosecutors used a Civil War–era statute to try Allen on "maiming by mob" charges. The irony of the charge is that the "Maiming by Mob" law had been put on the Virginia books to help protect blacks from lynching by whites.

"That charge took something out of the whole community," said Butch Harper, who ran the youth leagues that Allen first played in. "Allen had taken the local high school to the state championships in football and basketball. Seeing this happen to him was a travesty.

"Blacks felt that if a white boy had done the things Allen had done, he'd have been riding on the shoulders of the community, not going to its jail."

As expected, Allen's trial was a lightning rod for racial tensions. There were allegations made from the black community that the presiding judge was a friend of the family of one of the victims. Some witnesses said the fight started when racial remarks were hurled at Allen and his friends, but others said they never heard them.

During the trial, one witness said that he and a group of white men from nearby Poquoson were finishing a night of bowling when Allen, who was approaching the snack bar, said, "What's your problem? What are you looking at?"

The witness said his group told Allen that they didn't want any trouble, but one of Allen's friends, Michael Simmons, punched him in the back of the head. Allen denied the accusation, saying that as he approached the snack bar, one of the men from Poquoson shouted a racial slur at him and called him a "little boy."

Other witnesses said that confrontation led to the brawl between Allen and his friends and the group of white men from Poquoson. Chairs were allegedly thrown by both groups and three people were injured. Then witnesses said the fight stopped, but started up again after a woman confronted Allen's group.

A bowling alley employee identified Allen as the person who hit him with a chair, and prosecutors said that several black witnesses also identified Allen as the primary culprit.

"I had to sit there and listen to people lie, and nothin' I could do about it," Allen said of his trial. "I mean, I come in to the bowling alley with one guy and pretty soon I'm linked with fifteen, twenty guys."

Allen's status as a great basketball player also hurt him.

During his trial, Nike sent Allen, who had been the MVP at five of its basketball camps, airline tickets to a camp in Indianapolis so that he would not miss any activities while his trial was in progress. This was a terrible public relations move because it gave the public the impression that not only did Allen not care about his trial but that he thought he was somehow above the law.

In the closing arguments, prosecutors used Nike's famous slogan "Just Do It" while asking jurors to find Allen guilty. What role the trip to the Nike camp had in influencing the jury is not known, but on September 8, 1993, Allen was found guilty of maiming by mob.

The final blow came at Allen's sentencing. Although seventeen years old, Allen had been tried as an adult. And even though Allen had no previous criminal record, Judge Nelson Overton sentenced him to fifteen years, ten of which were suspended.

Allen was placed in shackles and taken to the Newport News City Farm to begin a five-year prison term that would have effectively ended his dreams and his plans to save his family.

"It hurts to look back and remember that Allen was seventeen years old and being tried as an adult," Coach Bailey said. "I sent him to that bowling alley that night just to have fun.

"My wife and I, even now, can lay down, close our eyes, and cry again."

Allen Iverson was in jail for a crime he felt he didn't commit.

His dreams of becoming an NBA player seemed as if they were over, but Allen didn't fall into despair.

"There was no lights, sometimes no water, no heat, nothing to eat," Allen said. "I was in jail. That was the thing that hurt me the most out of everything.

"Part of me being in there. I was never scared. I was never intimidated by anybody in there. I just knew I had to get out of the predicament I was in and do something for my family."

Billy Payne, the warden at Newport News City Farm at that time, said that Allen was a model prisoner.

"I found him to be an exceptional young man," Payne said of Allen. "He knew where he wanted to go and how he wanted to get there. Many people in the community felt he had been treated unfairly. I imagine Allen felt the same way, but I never once heard him complain."

Allen held on to his dreams, but he knew that colleges were not going to recruit him while he was in jail.

"I'm sure some colleges will stay away," Iverson once said in an interview from his jail cell. "But it'll work out.

This has given me time to think about what I need to do to succeed in the world."

Fortunately for Allen, there were people on the outside who supported him. A group of three attorneys worked his appeals case, and after Allen had spent four months in jail, then–Virginia governor L. Douglas Wilder awarded him conditional clemency. The condition being that Allen could not play organized sports until he graduated from high school. That meant no senior seasons in either football or basketball.

Sue Lambiotte was another person who saw something special in Allen. She had agreed to work with him as a non-paid tutor while he was in prison and continued to do so after his release. She accepted no excuses from Allen for not showing up, not having his homework, or not getting his classwork done.

"That was probably worse than jail for Allen," Lambiotte once said in an interview. "But he kept coming."

Allen came to Lambiotte's learning center for the last time on September 22, 1994. When Allen passed his final test that day, she had a graduation ceremony for him. He was the class valedictorian.

"I asked Allen one time, 'Did God make a mistake with you?' Maybe he was given too much for one person to handle.

"He's been blessed with so many tremendous skills, and so many opportunities, that I had to ask him that question.

"People know he's a great basketball player, but they don't know that when he got out of jail and he was in school (Richard Milburn High School), Allen taught our art class. He's a fabulous artist.

"He's also an excellent writer and a superb thinker. He's extremely patient and slow to speak, but he has something to say when he answers. But only if he trusts you. If he doesn't, he won't say a word."

Finally, two years after Allen was released from prison, his conviction was overturned by the Virginia state court of appeals due to insufficient evidence.

"You take a hundred kids, give them Allen's athletic talent, and put the same set of obstacles in their path, I guarantee you every one of them will fall down and not get up," Allen's high school football coach, Dennis Kozlowski, said. "Allen gets up, no matter what. He's the most resilient person I have ever known."

Officially, Allen was exonerated from the crime, and there is no record of his ever being convicted of it. But Allen will always know the truth.

"I've seen the bad side of life and I survived," Allen said. "My past has taught me a lot, and I'm not ashamed of it. It taught me how quickly things can be taken away from you.

"It taught me how important it is to believe in yourself even if others turn their back on you. It wasn't easy waking up in a cell. But it would've been easier to quit. I didn't do that. I fought through the hard times."

And into the darkness of Allen's life came a light.

His name was John Thompson. His offer to Allen Iverson was Georgetown University.

4 | Along Came a Hoya

Everyone knew that Bethel star Allen Iverson was one of the best high school basketball players in the country. But following his conviction, and despite the fact that Allen had been granted clemency and was out of prison, most of the top college programs decided the situation surrounding him made him too controversial to recruit.

Fortunately, Georgetown University basketball coach John Thompson was a 6-foot-10 African-American man who wasn't scared of anything. He had played basketball at Providence College in the early 1960s, when integration between black and white athletes was still frowned upon by a lot of Americans. He also won an NBA Championship as a member of the 1965 Boston Celtics.

Coach Thompson had taken over the basketball program at Georgetown, a tiny Catholic university in Washington, D.C., and turned it into a national power, and became the first African-American to coach an NCAA Division I Basketball Champion when his Hoyas won in 1983.

Coach Thompson had had his own share of headlines. Although he claimed it was untrue, many critics said that Coach Thompson recruited only African-American players to Georgetown, which was a predominantly white college. Others said that Coach Thompson used his size to intimidate other coaches and the media, and that he ran his program in a cloak of secrecy. ("Hoya Paranoia" became the unkind phrase used to describe Georgetown's basketball program.)

But Coach Thompson cared deeply about his players. Many had come from impoverished backgrounds with no positive male role model in their lives. Treating his players like his sons, Coach Thompson instilled a sense of discipline and determination that would help them succeed in life even if basketball was taken away.

He was an educator and a father before he was a coach.

One dramatized story says that Ann Iverson, desperately fearing for her son's future, came crying to Coach Thompson and begged him to take Allen and give him some of the "tough love" for which Georgetown basketball had become famous. But regardless of how it came about, Coach Thompson decided that Allen was indeed worth giving an opportunity and signed him to a letter of intent on April 19, 1994.

"I don't have any concerns about Allen because Allen would not be here if I had concerns about him," Coach Thompson said back in 1994. "I've said many times that I don't want any jackasses. We're not a program for problem people."

Instead, Georgetown was a program for great basketball

players as evidenced by the fact that its alumni included NBA stars Eric "Sleepy" Floyd, Patrick Ewing, Reggie Williams, Alonzo Mourning, and Dikembe Mutombo. But of all of the great players that had come through the Georgetown program, there had never been one like Allen Iverson.

A change in his furlough program from prison allowed Allen to join other recruits and play in Washington's Kenner League basketball program in the summer of 1994. Playing his first organized basketball in more than a year, Allen totaled 99 points in three games.

In Allen's first game as a Hoya, a preseason game against the Fort Hood Tankers, a team of Texas-based soldiers, he scored 36, had five assists, and three steals in just 23 minutes of action.

"I saw Lew Alcindor, Austin Carr, Moses Malone, Alonzo Mourning, Albert King, Ralph Sampson, and Patrick Ewing play in high school," *Washington Post* columnist Thomas Boswell wrote after seeing Iverson for the first time in 1994. "Now, I have two memories on my first-impression top shelf. Lew Alcindor (the man who became Kareem Abdul-Jabbar) and Allen Iverson. Ewing is now third."

Allen displayed the uncanny quickness, ball-handling skills, and scoring ability that had made him a high school All-America and would eventually make him the No. 1 overall pick in the 1996 NBA Draft.

"He did all the things within the flow of the game," former Georgetown center and current NBA player Don Reid said of Allen back in 1994. "What has impressed me the most was his penetrating and pitching. Looking down low for the big men after he has drawn our men away from us. As a big man, that makes you very happy."

Allen's skills were so overwhelming that Coach Thompson actually changed his style of play to accommodate his new star. With centers like Ewing, Mourning, and Mutombo headlining his previous teams, Coach Thompson had always played a defensive, disciplined, slow-down game.

With Allen as the focal point, Coach Thompson pushed down hard on the pedal of a Ferrari.

"You don't want to control the Allen Iversons of the world," Coach Thompson said years later about his philosophy with Allen. "You want to get a quarter horse, you get a quarter horse. You want a racehorse, you get a racehorse. Allen's a racehorse. You don't change him. He's too talented.

"You utilize his style of play. Too many people are trying to change Allen and worry about his style of play. It's almost like getting a high-speed car and slowing it down. Buy a slower car."

On the court, Allen's freshman year was everything he and Coach Thompson could have hoped for. He got Allen to play a controlled game within a team framework without sacrificing his dynamic individual skills.

In Allen's first collegiate game, Georgetown faced defending NCAA Champion Arkansas, which came into the season ranked No. 1 and favored to repeat. The young Hoyas lost 104–80 with Allen scoring 19 points on 5-for-18 shooting with 8 turnovers. His numbers weren't great, but Allen's uncanny skills were unmistakable.

"I've been to three calf shows, nine horse ropings, and seen Elvis once," University of Arkansas coach Nolan Richardson said after Allen's collegiate debut. "But I've never seen anything like this in my life."

Of course, there were critics. CBS television college basketball analyst Billy Packer wasted no time ripping into Allen's first performance as a college player.

"Based on the performance I saw," Packer said. "(Allen Iverson) has no comprehension how to be a basketball player. I saw (then boxing world champion) Pernell 'Sweetpea' Whitaker fight when he was a teenager. He obviously had all the raw skills. He took those skills and refined them. Now he's pound-for-pound the best fighter in the world.

"Where Allen is, he's got all the skills, but now he has to learn how to be a basketball player. That's not to say he won't get some incredible stats. But that doesn't mean he's an accomplished basketball player."

For his part, Allen never said he was an accomplished player after just one game, but he liked his teacher and thought he was on the right path.

"Coach Thompson is the one that really taught me how to play basketball," Allen said. "I still don't know it like I want to, but he gave me a clear picture of how to play the game."

After more than a year away from organized basketball, Allen was starting to roll and the Hoyas went with him. The loss to Arkansas was followed by a twelve-game winning streak that had Georgetown ranked tenth in the country. Thirteen games into his collegiate career Allen was averaging 20.7 points, 4.4 assists, and 3.3 steals a game.

"He's spectacular," Providence College coach Pete Gillen said after Allen torched his Friars for 30 points in his first Big East Conference game. "Allen Iverson will choreograph many happy moments for Georgetown."

Coach Thompson had a funny take on Allen's quick start.

"It has been said that Allen can leap tall buildings in a single bound," Coach Thompson said. "That's not true. That being said, there's no question that he's definitely a special talent."

Allen was taking all of the early attention in stride, never getting too big-headed about his abilities.

"I just play," Allen said after he had been named Big East Rookie of the Week four times in six weeks. "I don't even get involved in any of that type of talk. It's the people in the stands and my coaches who determine how well I'm playing. I just go out there night in and night out and give 110 percent. I've gotten used to the publicity by now."

But there was a darker side to what was going on with Allen. His background was well documented and that made him an easy target for fans who were determined to be cruel to the young star. During several road Big East games, fans held up signs calling Allen a criminal and chanted "Jailbird" at him. They called Allen "O.J.," and sometimes the bands played "Jailhouse Rock" during time-outs.

This was one battle Allen would not have to fight. Coach Thompson was going to do it for him.

Coach Thompson had been through this before. Patrick Ewing had grown up in Jamaica and spoke with a heavy accent. Some fans cruelly held signs that said "Patrick Ewing Can't Read Dis!" and others referred to him as a monkey. The Georgetown coach had waited patiently for Big East officials to do the right thing and stop the offensive abuse of Patrick, but when they didn't act on their own, he forced their hand by threatening to take his basketball team off the court.

A decade later the same thing was happening again.

On January 23, in a game against Villanova in Philadelphia at the Spectrum, Coach Thompson said if a few knuckleheads in the crowd of 17,332 were not made to take down signs referring to Allen's criminal conviction, Georgetown would not take the court. The cruelest sign referred to Allen as the next Michael Jordan, but Jordan's name was crossed out and replaced by that of O.J. Simpson, who was about to go on trial for double-murder in Los Angeles.

"There are some things you have to accept, but that's not one of them," Coach Thompson said. "You accept certain ribbing, but there is a line. I should not have to be the one to point that out. I can't condone any Christian university (Villanova) sitting and watching that happen, whether it's Georgetown or someone else. If that happens, I'm going to walk. It's that simple. That's what I said to (Villanova officials)."

Eventually, Villanova coach Steve Lappas went into the crowd. He said, "I told them if anybody holds up a sign like that again, I'm kicking them out. It's one thing to yell for an opponent to miss a shot, but there's no place in college basketball for stuff like that. Unfortunately, you can have 17,000 good fans, but there's still going to be a few morons."

Coach Thompson's power-play worked, and from then on, Allen was only treated to the typical fan razzing at visiting courts.

But Coach Thompson's protection of Allen wasn't limited to fans. The media had to watch its words whenever it dealt with Georgetown players. Asking questions about basketball was fine. Asking questions about other stuff definitely was not. During the NCAA Tournament, when a reporter asked Allen if he could answer some questions about his legal troubles, Coach Thompson stopped Allen and said, "No, he can't. He's a child. We're here to talk about basketball. How would you like it if I asked you about your children, your family, your wife?"

Allen averaged 20.4 points to finish fourth in the Big East Conference in scoring. He led the league with 3.0 steals a game. He also averaged 4.42 assists a game. Allen was named the Big East Rookie of the Year and Defensive Player of the Year.

The Hoyas finished 21-10 and advanced to the Sweet 16 of the NCAA Tournament for the first time since 1989.

During the summer of 1995, Allen represented the United States at the World University Games in Japan. Playing with future NBA stars like Milwaukee Buck Ray Allen, San Antonio Spur Tim Duncan, and New Jersey Net Kerry Kittles, Allen led the team in scoring (16.7 ppg), assists (6.1), and steals (3.0). He shot 56 percent from the floor as the USA won the gold medal.

Off the court, Coach Thompson finally provided the authoritative male figure that Allen had wanted in his life.

"Coach Thompson was like a father figure to me, right

off hand," Allen said after his freshman season. "It just clicked. Ninety percent of having a relationship with him is things that occur off-court.

"He helped me. I didn't want to go to Georgetown and just do anything. Any problems that I have, I can go to him and he'll sit down and listen It's a lot more than player-coach between us. I don't think I could have made it through last year without him."

Coach Thompson said his relationship with Allen was about being an educator and a parent.

"If you've been in this business for a while," Coach Thompson said back then, "you know you're not supposed to be impressed with people. You're here to attempt to mold and get students prepared for their next stage of life. That's what education is all about. Allen has done just that. He's done what I've asked him to do, and when he has not done it, we've sat down and talked about it.

"Allen wants to educate himself. So it's not a problem. It's almost amusing to me sometimes to hear the questions I'm asked about him in relation to the person that I have to deal with."

There was also good news for Allen on the legal front. Although he had received clemency from Virginia governor L. Douglas Wilder after his conviction for maiming by mob, Allen's lawyers had worked continuously to have the 1993 verdict overturned.

On June 20, 1995, the Virginia Court of Appeals set aside the convictions of Allen, Samuel Wynn, and Michael Simmons. The three-judge appeals court panel agreed with Allen's attorneys who argued that there was no evidence that Allen joined in any mob that might have been formed during the fight.

"It goes without saying we're very happy with the fact that Allen has an opportunity to continue his life, be a successful student and a successful citizen afterwards," Coach Thompson said.

"When I first met Allen, I told him my biggest concern was not about his ability to play, but that he had felony charges hanging over his head. The real end of the story will be what he does with this opportunity from here."

The saga truly ended for Allen on July 26, 1995, when prosecutors in Hampton decided not to retry him on the charges relating to the bowling alley brawl.

"A retrial would retard, rather than advance that maturation toward becoming productive and solid citizens," Commonwealth's attorney Christopher W. Hutton wrote. "The defendants have made marked progress toward educational and/or employment goals. The Commonwealth would seek retrial of these charges had the defendants not made this progress."

Through his lawyer, Thomas B. Shuttleworth, Allen issued a statement saying, "I am delighted that the decision has been made that there will not be any further court proceedings in my case. This is a tremendous relief to me and my family."

Still, as Allen often likes to say, "Things weren't all peaches and cream."

For Allen, life at Georgetown presented everything he'd dreamed of, a nice place to sleep, three square meals a day, a safe environment with no drugs, violence, or guns.

"It's real fun," Allen said about being a freshman at Georgetown. "The best part of it is learning from my teammates. They've been through a lot more than me."

But the fun always ended when he left campus. It took Allen only about two hours to get home to Hampton from Washington, D.C. Whenever he returned home, it was to the Stewart Garden Apartments, where his mother and two sisters were still living in "the sewer."

It was more than Allen could stand. He knew he had to take care of things soon.

5 | I'm Going Pro

It was just after Game 2 of the NBA Finals and the Sixers had lost a heartbreaker to the Los Angeles Lakers. Allen Iverson had turned twenty-six the day before and losing wasn't a gift he much wanted.

As Allen sat in front of the media to answer questions, he carried his two-year-old son, Allen II (called Deuce), in his right arm, while his five-year-old daughter, Tiaura, sat on his left knee.

It was nine P.M. in Los Angeles, but Deuce was still operating on East Coast time. To Deuce it was midnight and well past his bedtime. He was asleep with his tiny head snuggled in his father's chest. Tiaura had more stamina. She listened intently as Dad answered questions.

"My bad kids, man," Allen said of Tiaura and Deuce. "I've got two bad kids, two spoiled kids. But that's the way I want it. I just want them to grow up better than I did. I want them to have the things that I didn't have, but I want them to still have my heart. I want them to be hard as steel, just

41

like I am, and be able to overcome some of the obstacles they're going to face in their lives."

Family has always been the guiding force in Allen's life. As his biological father had abandoned him, and his surrogate father had spent time in prison, Allen had assumed the pressures of being the man of the house for his mother and two little sisters.

"There are some things that change you as you grow and get some success," Allen said. "You have to be more responsible for what you do, and people put pressures on you.

"But some things never change. My family is still the most important thing to me. They motivate me."

Allen had made it through being put in prison for four months and been given a scholarship to play basketball at Georgetown University. But whenever he went back home, he saw that his mother, Ann, and sisters, Brandy and Iiesha, were still living in poverty in Hampton's Stewart Garden Apartments.

Allen desperately wanted to get them out of those dreadful living conditions. Iiesha's seizures had generated medical bills that had pushed the family toward bankruptcy.

But in 1995 Allen would find out what it was like to become a real father himself. His longtime girlfriend, Tawanna Turner, became pregnant and gave birth to their daughter, Tiaura.

Now Allen felt he not only had to take care of his mother and sisters, he had to make it to the NBA to take care of his girlfriend and daughter.

"Family means everything to me," Allen said. "My family gets knocked down, I'm picking them up if I can. That's just the way I am. I cherish my family."

For the first time in his life, while he was at Georgetown, Allen was able to just be a young man and do carefree things that other people his age got to do.

Allen was happy at Georgetown, maybe happier than he had ever been, but he knew he couldn't stay. Responsibility to his family came first.

By the start of Allen's sophomore year at Georgetown, speculation had already begun that the lightning-quick, high-scoring point guard was going to declare himself eligible for the 1996 NBA Draft at the end of the college season.

Up until that time, no Hoya had ever left Coach Thompson's program early to turn professional—not Patrick Ewing, who would eventually become a No. 1 overall selection in 1985; not Reggie Williams, No. 4 overall in 1987; not Dikembe Mutombo, No. 4 in 1991; and not Alonzo Mourning, No. 2 overall in 1992.

And the way Coach Thompson saw it, Allen Iverson was not going to be the first Georgetown player to turn professional early, either—unless *he* decided Allen should go.

"If Allen Iverson leaves, be assured I have told him to go, or he will go nowhere," Coach Thompson said as Georgetown's 1996 regular season was winding down.

Coach Thompson said he was angry that all of the talk about Allen leaving early was putting an unacceptable burden on the young player.

"I think it's unfair to Allen, a first-generation student in college, a young man who has been through a lot of suffering," Coach Thompson said.

College basketball had become an unscrupulous business with friends, hangers-on, and other outside influences always telling the best players that they should leave college as soon as possible and take the millions of dollars that the NBA offered.

Coach Thompson had seen all of the signs before, and he was determined to protect Allen and allow him to make a decision based on what he wanted to do himself, not what others told him he should do.

"The wolves are circling the house now," Coach Thompson said. "The buzzards are flying over the top, and I start getting attitude because you've got to get ready for the wolves.

"I'm confident that Allen's decision is not going to be a mystery to me. That's not going to be something that I'm worrying about. Allen's not going anyway, unless I tell him that it's time for him to go. And tomorrow I may tell him it's time to go, but I doubt it."

Still, even as Coach Thompson spoke, there were signs that Allen had already made his decision to leave for the NBA. Since early April of 1996, Allen had been seen driving a $130,000 Mercedes Benz on loan from a dealer.

Considering Allen's financial background, having the car was clearly going to be difficult for him to explain should National Collegiate Athletic Association officials decide to investigate him.

The loan of the car would have likely put Allen's collegiate eligibility in question were he to return to Georgetown.

"(The Mercedes) came from my sister," Allen said of the luxury car. "I was using the car just to get back and forth from home. (The dealer) let me keep it, I guess, longer than they'd let anybody else keep it."

If the speculation was a distraction off the court, it certainly didn't affect Allen's performance on it. In fact, the way Allen played further fueled the thought that he would be a high draft pick, perhaps the first overall.

His game had become more well rounded and complete between his freshman and sophomore years.

"A lot of times I got caught up in the hype of the game and got out of control," Allen said. "Now, I'm working hard on being patient, a lot more than I was last year. I made a lot of freshman-type mistakes, but I matured as the season went on, and learned a lot of things from game to game.

"That's the thing Coach talks to me about now, the leadership role and being able to run this team. The point guard position is supposed to be the focal point and run the show and that's what I have to do for this team and if I want to ever think about playing at the next level."

Allen finished his sophomore season averaging 24.7 points, 5.0 assists, 3.8 rebounds, and 3.5 steals. He was once again named Big East Conference Defensive Player of the Year, and was a First Team All-America.

In the Sweet 16 of the NCAA Tournament, Allen scored 32 with 4 rebounds, 5 assists, and 5 steals, and Georgetown beat Texas Tech to advance to the Elite Eight.

"We didn't apply as much pressure in the post as we might have, but that might have been because we had such awareness of Iverson," Texas Tech coach James Dickey said of his team's defeat. "You always have to be conscious of where he is on the court."

With a chance for Georgetown to advance to the 1996 Final Four, Allen scored 23, but the Hoyas lost to top-ranked Massachusetts and Player of the Year Marcus Camby.

If Allen had any second thoughts about going to the NBA, it only took another trip home to Hampton to erase them. Iiesha's seizures were continuing. That and the thought of caring for his own one-year-old baby girl, Tiaura, convinced him it was time for him to use his God-given abilities to make some money and fulfill his plan.

On May 1, 1996, Allen and Georgetown University called a press conference. Everyone knew what it was about.

Citing personal and financial reasons, Allen became the first player in Coach Thompson's twenty-four years at Georgetown to leave early for the NBA.

"After carefully weighing my options with Coach Thompson and my family, I've decided to enter the NBA Draft," Allen said, accompanied by his mother Ann. "I definitely plan to further my education, but my family needs to be addressed right now. My baby sister was having some medical problems, and I think that really pushed me out the door. Now I can get a specialist for her, and help my mom along. She raised me for twenty years, did the best she could, and I just want the opportunity to do the best for her."

Coach Thompson was disappointed to lose a great player, but he fully supported Allen's decision.

"I think it would be a little bit stupid of me to try and change a man who can think and make judgments," Coach

Thompson said at Allen's announcement. "Or for me to try to persuade him or try to con him from doing something that he feels in his heart he must do. If you were to ask me, 'Should he stay here?' I would tell you absolutely yes. If you were to ask me, 'Did he make the right decision to leave?' I would tell you absolutely yes, based on the reasons he used to make that decision."

Both Allen and Coach Thompson said NCAA rules that prevented athletes from earning money by getting jobs or stopped schools from helping athletes with serious financial hardships made it impossible for poor athletes to stay in school when they could help ease the burdens facing their families.

"I don't blame anybody but us," Coach Thompson said of collegiate athletics. "We have the most antiquated set of rules. It's a frustrating thing. Even though (Georgetown) might have the best hospital around, we couldn't do anything (to help Allen's sister). If we don't look at it very clearly, there won't be one halfway sensible reason why kids will stay in school."

Allen said his decision came down to making money for his family.

"If my situation at home had permitted me to stay in school, if I had been well off, I think I would have stayed," Allen said. "I didn't have any problems with the college life. Coach Thompson is a great coach.

"He taught me a lot of things, on and off the court. There are so many things you can learn in college, especially when you have a coach like Coach Thompson. A lot of times I felt like it was fifty percent basketball and fifty percent real life, when he would call you to the side and talk about things like what I was getting ready to deal with right now.

"He talked, prepared me for that. I think two more years would even prepare me a lot more. But this is something I had to do. Everyone was depending on me. My mother, my sister, my daughter."

But the decision wasn't without its problems. Allen hadn't turned twenty-one, and he had entered a man's world where basketball wasn't just a game anymore—it was a multibillion-dollar business. Also, Coach Thompson would no longer be there to shelter Allen. Allen was going to be rich, and there are many pitfalls, temptations, and traps for a young man who is suddenly given millions of dollars.

"I have concerns about Allen's ability emotionally and psychologically to deal with the things the NBA relates to," Coach Thompson said after Allen's announcement. "In his basketball ability I have the ultimate amount of confidence. I'm scared about the other twenty-two hours."

Although he played just two seasons and sixty-seven games at Georgetown, Allen finished tenth on the Hoyas all-time scoring list with 1,539 points. His career scoring average of 23.0 points is the highest in Georgetown history, nearly six points a game better than Eric "Sleepy" Floyd.

The 926 points Allen scored in his sophomore season was more than 120 points better than Reggie Williams (802) scored in the 1986–87 season.

Allen finished twelfth in all-time assists (307) and third in steals (213). His 124 steals in the 1995–96 season was a one-season record.

"I wouldn't be sitting here today if it wasn't for the problems at home," Allen said as he left Georgetown. "I loved Georgetown, and I loved playing college basketball. But there are times in life you've got to make decisions, so I made mine.

"If I lacked the abilities, I definitely wouldn't have come out for the NBA, but we all know that is not a problem. Like I said, I'm ready."

6 | What's the Point—Guard?

Once Allen Iverson made the decision to leave Georgetown University and enter the 1996 NBA Draft, the next challenge was to become the first overall selection.

That pick belonged to the Philadelphia 76ers, who were one of the worst teams in the league and at that time hadn't had a winning campaign since the 1991–92 season.

In the NBA the thirteen teams that did not make the playoffs the previous season are entered into a draft lottery. Each team receives a certain number of Ping-Pong balls based on its record—the one with the most losses gets the most picks. The top three picks in the draft are then randomly drawn out of a barrel.

In 1996, because the Toronto Raptors and Vancouver Grizzlies were expansion teams, only the top pick was selected by the lottery. The Sixers won the first pick, with Toronto selecting second and Vancouver third.

So why were Allen Iverson and all of the other prospects so anxious to come to Philadelphia? Simple: In 1996 being the first overall pick meant a three-year contract worth $9.39 million.

The further a player slipped in the draft, the more money it would cost him in his first contract.

"Being picked first is important to me because I feel that I'm the best player in the draft," Allen said as he prepared for the 1996 draft. "No player in the draft should think another player is better than they are. It'll be a great honor to be picked No. 1. Also, I want to be close to my family. Philadelphia is close enough."

With Villanova University being a Big East rival of Georgetown, the fans in Philadelphia had seen Allen up close in action in both of his collegiate seasons. If it had been up to the fans to make the choice, Allen would have been the runaway winner.

But the Sixers were an organization in transition.

Longtime owner Harold Katz had just sold the team, and a vibrant, dynamic team president named Pat Croce was given the responsibility of rebuilding this once proud organization.

Croce, who was the physical trainer for the Sixers when they won the NBA title in 1983, had hired a first-time general manager in Brad Greenberg, who in turn hired a rookie coach named Johnny Davis. These three men, who were all rookies in their positions, were going to make the most important draft decision for the Sixers in a decade.

They had to get it right.

"We've got a lot of options," Greenberg said at the time. "We want to make the right choice."

And as good as Allen was, this particular draft was the

best since 1984, the year in which Hakeem Olajuwon, Michael Jordan, Sam Perkins, and Charles Barkley were all selected within the first five picks.

In addition to Allen, the 1996 draft class included University of Massachusetts forward/center and National Player of the Year Marcus Camby; Big East Player of the Year and University of Connecticut guard Ray Allen; Georgia Tech freshman sensation Stephon Marbury; University of California freshman Shareef Abdur-Rahim; University of Kentucky sophomore sensation Antoine Walker, and a seventeen-year-old phenom from Lower Merion High School named Kobe Bryant.

The year before, the Sixers had drafted University of North Carolina shooting guard Jerry Stackhouse, and their primary needs in 1996 were a center and a point guard. Since there was no dominating center such as a Shaquille O'Neal in this draft, the belief was that the Sixers decision was going to be between Allen and Stephon Marbury.

Although he averaged fewer assists than Allen (4.5 a game compared to 4.7), 6-foot-2 Stephon Marbury was considered a more advanced point guard coming out of college.

Stephon, from Coney Island, New York, was the latest in a strong tradition of Georgia Tech point guards that included NBA players Mark Price, Kenny Anderson, and Travis Best. Although just a freshman, Stephon, then nineteen years old, was a third-team All-America, and just the fifth freshman in Atlantic Coast Conference history to be named first-team All-ACC.

"I wouldn't say I'm better suited [for the Sixers than Iverson]," Stephon said. "I'm not even going to get into comparing Allen and myself. I can tell you what I do. I make every player around me better.

"I know that I can get (Sixers Jerry Stackhouse and Derrick Coleman) easier baskets than they have been getting. I know that on transition I can make a lot of easy baskets for my teammates.

"I'm not too flashy, but I can be when I want to be or need to be. I don't think point guards are made. I think point guards are born. I think I've been delivered to be a point guard."

In contrast, there was no question that Allen's primary thought was to be a scorer rather than a playmaker. But because of his 6-foot-0, 165-pound frame, he was determined that he was going to have to play the No. 1 position in the NBA.

The league just didn't have a strong track record for successful six-foot shooting guards.

"I'm only six feet tall," Allen said. "I'm going to have to play point guard. That's the position I think I'm best at. I think my talent enables me to score, but I think I can run the point as well.

"I feel that Stephon is a great player, and he's going to get a lot better in the future. I'm going to be the same way. I think I could come to Philadelphia and do a good job, but Stephon could as well. Who's it going to be? I don't know. I just know I would love to go there."

Still, the skepticism about Allen's ability to play the point remained. The Sixers had to wonder if he could coexist with Jerry Stackhouse, an explosive scorer who needed to take a lot of shots, and the enigmatic Derrick Coleman, whose questionable work ethic prevented him from maximizing his enormous talent.

Allen was aware of what was being said about him, and he was aware of the potential harm if the Sixers started listening. He went on the offensive.

"At Georgetown, Coach Thompson wanted me to score and put the ball up," Allen said of his shoot-first mentality. "That's something I had to do. But it would be ridiculous for me to think I would come into Philadelphia and try to do all of the scoring.

"Derrick Coleman needs the ball. Jerry Stackhouse is a fantastic player. It would be outrageous for me to go to the Sixers and think I'm going to shoot the ball a lot. By simply playing with them, my assists would go up tremendously.

"The NBA is more suited to me than the college game. It's all man-to-man defense in the NBA, which is how I like to play."

Less than three weeks before the draft, the Sixers still hadn't given a clear sign whether their preference was Allen or Stephon.

"(Stephon and Allen) are both good point guards," said Sixers player personnel assistant Maurice Cheeks, who started at that position for the Sixers' 1983 championship team. "We're going to look around and see who's the best player for us.

"You learn all kinds of things once you get to the NBA. Certain things you did in college, you won't necessarily do in the NBA. If these are great, true point guards, hopefully, they'll be the same in the NBA."

Even though the draft night hadn't come yet, Allen was already reaping the rewards of his decision to turn professional.

Georgetown coach John Thompson got Allen to sign with super-agent David Falk, who not only represented the Georgetown coach, but superstars like Michael Jordan, Patrick Ewing, Dikembe Mutombo, and Alonzo Mourning.

The first thing Falk did was negotiate a multimillion-dollar endorsement contract for Allen with Reebok.

"My marketing is going really well right now," Allen said.

7 | Hi, I'm Pat Croce

Back in 1986 the NBA Draft had been predicted to be one of the best ever in NBA history. Sadly it turned out to be cursed. Two days after he was drafted second overall by the Boston Celtics, University of Maryland star Len Bias died of cocaine intoxication. In addition, Chris Washburn, the third pick, William Bedford, the sixth pick, and Roy Tarpley, the seventh pick, would all have their NBA careers shortened due to drug and alcohol abuse.

The tragedy of 1986 caused NBA teams to reevaluate how they went about selecting players in whom they were going to invest millions of dollars. Suddenly character became an important factor in the evaluation process, and teams started hiring private investigators to do thorough background checks on the players they were considering drafting.

In 1996, Allen Iverson, because of his history, was the subject of many investigations, though in fairness, the Sixers retained private investigators to look into the backgrounds of Allen, Stephon Marbury, and Marcus Camby.

The brawl at the bowling alley was not the only brush with trouble Allen had been in while in high school. He had been cited for driving without a license, after which he failed to show up for several court dates. And he had been present at a party at a hotel in which a man was shot and killed.

"You want to make sure that trouble in the past is not trouble in the present," Sixers president Pat Croce said at the time.

Pat Croce is a Philadelphian all the way through.

A health and fitness guru, he was a physical trainer for the Philadelphia 76ers and Philadelphia Flyers in the 1980s. A savvy businessman and dynamic personality, Croce created Sports Physical Therapists, a sports medicine empire with forty centers in eleven states. After selling his company, Croce, in 1996, helped arranged the deal that got longtime 76ers owner Harold Katz to sell the team to Flyers owner Ed Snider and his new partner the Comcast Corporation.

The new venture—called Comcast-Spectator—consisted of the Flyers, the Sixes, the brand-new First Union Center, the First Union Spectrum, and a minor-league hockey team—the Philadelphia Phantoms.

Croce bought a small percentage of the Sixers and was named team president. His stated goal was to bring back the pride and passion of the Sixers by returning them to their championship form.

His first decision would be his biggest—whether or not to make Allen Iverson the first overall pick in the draft.

Like the other top prospects, Allen had come to Philadelphia to work out for the Sixers. His skill grades were off the chart. He had a 40.5-inch vertical jump and a 45-inch jump with a running start.

Croce, who wasn't present for Allen's workout, said that Sixers Hall of Famer Julius "Dr. J" Erving was the only other person he had ever seen clear the 40-inch barrier.

But an amazing workout by Allen wasn't going to be enough by itself to convince Croce that Allen was the guy. He wanted to meet Allen face-to-face and have a heart-to-heart talk with him.

"The first time I met Allen was during an interview for the 1996 draft," Pat Croce remembered. "We had the first pick and we were either going to pick Allen, Marcus Camby, Stephon Marbury, or Ray Allen.

"I was supposed to meet Allen at the Embassy Suites Hotel down by the Philadelphia airport. I walk in and go to the counter, but I don't see him. So I look around and I see this kid—sleeping on a couch in the lobby. He's lounging and wearing sweats. It looks like Allen Iverson, but I'm not really sure. So I say, 'Excuse me, are you Allen Iverson?' He looks up and says, 'Yeah.' I said, 'Hi, I'm Pat Croce.'

"We went over to a table in the corner and just sat there and talked for an hour or two. His phone rang and it was his mother. I didn't mind him talking to his mother, and he didn't mind me hearing him talk to her."

The talk was graphic and straight to the point.

The Sixers knew about Michael Freeman, Allen's surrogate father, being arrested for selling cocaine, and Croce asked Allen straight up if he had ever done drugs.

"No," Allen said.

Croce, who grew up in the streets of South Philadelphia, knew the game. He challenged Allen's answer and said he didn't believe him.

He talked the talk with Allen, but Allen never faulted. He said he had never touched drugs.

"We got down and dirty," Croce said. "We got into all the past baggage."

After their talk Croce came away not just believing Allen but being impressed by him. Croce admired Allen's commitment to his family. He admired how Allen, even though he did not like that Freeman had been arrested, did not abandon the man he called his dad. He admired how Allen had visited Freeman in prison and, seeing the condition of his shoes, gave his sneakers to Freeman and went home barefoot. But mostly, Croce admired how Allen did not back away from his past and did not make excuses for growing up poor.

"My past taught me a lot," Allen said. "I'm not ashamed of how I had to grow up. It taught me how quickly things can be taken away from you. It taught me how important it is to believe in yourself even if others turn their back on you."

During his two-hour conversation with Allen, Croce tapped into the thing that Michael Bailey, Allen's basketball coach at Bethel High, had done so many years earlier.

"I told Allen that I'd never lie to him if he never lied to me," Croce said.

That was all Allen needed to hear from Croce.

"I felt comfortable (talking to Pat Croce) because he was

real," Allen said. "I wanted him to know who I was, and that gave me the opportunity to tell him who I was."

The Sixers had made their decision.

"We knew Allen was going to be the pick," Croce said, thinking back to 1996. "He had had his workout and it was phenomenal. Besides, I think if we didn't pick him, I would've been shot by the city. Everyone was calling me and saying 'Yo, Pat, Iverson. Yo, Pat, Iverson.' I thought my name had become Pat Iverson.

"I'm so proud of Allen. I've defended him from the beginning because I saw his heart. Yes, there were bad times and setbacks, but I knew that deep down he was a good guy. Certainly, his talent was phenomenal.

"He didn't have the tattoos he has now. He wasn't wearing cornrows back then. But I never cared if he wanted to change himself to not look like Michael Jordan. Allen had his own look. I'm someone who beats to my own drum, so I can relate to that. Regardless, you just saw something special in this guy. I had an affection for him from the very start. I loved his toughness. I loved his loyalty to his friends."

On June 26, 1996, at the Continental Airlines Arena in East Rutherford, New Jersey, it became official. Allen Iverson became the No. 1 overall pick in the NBA Draft.

8 | He's No. 1

The 1996 NBA Draft was at the Continental Airlines Arena in East Rutherford, New Jersey, but the Sixers held a draft party at the brand-new First Union Center in South Philadelphia.

There were six thousand fans in attendance at the party, and they let out a loud cheer five minutes before the draft when Greenberg, then Sixers general manager, told them they would indeed be getting Allen Iverson when NBA commissioner David Stern read the name of the Sixers' pick.

"We wanted to give them something to be excited about early," Greenberg said at the time. "They're great fans. We wanted to give them what they wanted."

Allen was in New Jersey, with his family and all of the other top draft picks, and then it happened.

Commissioner Stern walked to the podium and said to fifteen thousand fans at the Continental Airlines Arena and a national television audience, "With the first pick in the

1996 NBA Draft, the Philadelphia 76ers select Allen Iverson, sophomore guard from Georgetown."

Dressed in a stylish gray suit with a black-and-white print tie, plus all of his silver and gold accessories, Allen walked onto the stage to cheers of the crowd, shook commissioner Stern's hand, and was given a 76ers hat to wear.

A lifetime of struggle to overcome the odds culminated in this unforgettable moment of elation for Allen. His dreams had come true. His plan had been fulfilled.

Allen Iverson had made it to the NBA.

"Hello, Philadelphia," Allen said in an interview that was patched in to his new hometown fans at the First Union Center. "I really wanted to be in Philadelphia. I felt of all the teams, I wanted to play for the Sixers.

"It's a new organization. I'm new. I want to start a new era. I have a lot of energy, a lot of enthusiasm. I'm somebody who plays every game like it's the last game. You won't be sorry the Sixers took me."

For Allen, June 26, 1996, had become the most special day of his life. At 6-0, Allen became the shortest player ever drafted No.1 overall. With the exception of Earvin "Magic" Johnson, whose 6-9 size made him the most unique point guard in league history, Allen was the first guard drafted first since the Houston Rockets selected University of Maryland point guard John Lucas in 1976.

"I felt all along that I was the best player in the draft," Allen said. "People may have thought Philadelphia should have chosen someone else, but they'll never convince me of anything different.

"I truly feel that I deserve to be where I am right now. I

knew that good things would happen in life if I kept believing. Now I'll show the world that I deserve this chance."

The Sixers said their reasons for selecting Allen first and not making a trade were obvious, though there had been rumors that the Vancouver Grizzlies might trade for the top pick.

"It was very, very clear that the most talented player was Allen," Greenberg said. "Once we made that decision, we were not going to move the pick.

"Allen is a special athlete, a special competitor, mentally tough, resilient. That made it an easy decision. He was the most exciting player in college basketball.

"He can be the most exciting and most talented player at his position in the NBA someday. He brings a winning attitude. People say he's the fiercest competitor they've ever been around. He wants to win so badly. The only thing that might get him frustrated and angry is if his teammates don't feel the same way. We love that.

"When somebody plays to win every single possession, all-out, very few players do that. He can do anything he wants on the court. He wants to take the next step as a player."

Stephon Marbury was drafted fourth by the Milwaukee Bucks and then traded to the Minnesota Timberwolves. A rivalry between two of the best young players in the NBA was born that night of the draft.

"I didn't want to go anyplace where I wasn't wanted," said Stephon, who now plays for the Phoenix Suns. "The Sixers were obviously in love with Iverson. I understand that.

"He's great. But someday down the road we'll get it on.

We're both high picks in the draft. I'm happy, and I know he is."

The day after the draft Allen drove down to Philadelphia for his formal introduction news conference. He was given a miniature Liberty Bell from then Philadelphia Mayor Ed Rendell.

"I have to be prepared for anything," Allen told the media. "All I can do is work hard, play every game like it could be my last. That's all I owe myself. That's all I owe the fans."

Typically, Allen was asked about his past and if he thought some fans would hold it against him.

"I don't think the fans could tear me down," Allen responded. "There's more pressure out there than playing in a game. And playing basketball is what I like the most. I can accept praise. I can accept criticism."

At the time Allen had no idea how much criticism he was eventually going to take as he started his NBA career. But Pat Croce said he knew Allen, because of who he was and how he played, would quickly become a Philly favorite.

"Nothing with us will challenge what Allen has already gone through in his life," Croce said. "I have all the respect in the world for him, seeing where he is after the adversity he's been through.

"It's educated him, brought out a rare, special talent in him. He has a will to succeed. Philadelphia can be tough because fans want a winner. But if they can't have a winner, they want effort. You can say this is a city that eats its young, but if the young show that effort, it's not going to eat them up."

Effort on the court was never going to be an issue with Allen, but from his opening introduction to Philadelphia, there were hints of things that would eventually become sources of controversy in his career.

When Allen arrived in Philadelphia, he was not wearing the neat dress suit he wore at the NBA Draft. He was much more relaxed, wearing a Reebok sweatsuit. His limousine from New York had been caught in traffic, and he arrived nearly an hour late. And in addition to his family, Allen also brought with him some of his closest friends from Hampton. They were dressed in jeans and T-shirts and wore fat gold chains and headbands.

Andre "Arnie" Steele, Marlon Moore, Rahshaan "Rah" Langford, Eric Jackson, and Lamont "Gold" Melvin have been Allen's friends for as long as he can remember. While many people—fans and media—said that Allen's friends were going to bring him down, Allen never wavered in his loyalty to them.

They became nationally known as Allen's "posse."

"That's funny, I thought they were my friends," Allen would say about the criticism. "My friends made me. They're the ones who had something to do with keeping me alive on the streets before all of this.

"So you want to tell me that once I do something positive, they can't take a positive ride with me? That's ludicrous. I love those guys, and you know what? They care about me. My friends were with me when I was struggling, and they're still with me now. They are my family."

Despite the distractions of his image off the court, Allen was confident in his ability to help the Sixers right away on it.

"I don't think they would've brought me in if they didn't want me to contribute," Allen said. "I don't really feel I have to be slow-walked through the first season or the second season.

"I have to step in, just play my game, show everybody why I'm here.

"I wouldn't actually say I'm a savior. All the guys who step on the court with me will be the saviors. We're going to do everything we accomplish together."

But make no mistake, Allen had already decided what kind of impact he wanted to make on the league. He didn't shortchange himself. In 1996 Michael Jordan had already retired once, and it was clear that his career was starting to wind down. So were those of a lot of stars who had carried the NBA through the last decade.

A new crop of stars were entering the league. Allen left no doubt that he intended to be one of the brightest.

"That's not something I want the media to give me," Allen said of his aspirations to sit on the throne as the NBA's best. "I want to take it!

"When I hear who they're going to give it to, I just smile because I can't wait. I know they don't want me to be that man, but I'm going to take it. That's just another obstacle I have to jump to show the people that they can believe in me. And to let the people know it's okay to dream.

"I want to be remembered as the best player in the NBA. That's a big statement, but I'm willing to try and back it up. I want to be the greatest basketball player. That's some big words, but that's the challenge of my life. Maybe people won't consider me the best, maybe some will. Who knows? I mean, the sky's the limit."

*   *   *

As the first pick in the draft, Allen received a three-year contract worth a guaranteed $9.386 million, with a starting salary of $2.72 million.

That alone wasn't bad for a kid who up to that point had lived in a house that occasionally leaked raw sewage into the floor, but Allen's contract with the Sixers was just the beginning of his newfound riches. His agent, David Falk, who had negotiated Michael Jordan's deal with Nike, negotiated a multimillion-dollar deal with Reebok for Allen.

Reebok was not overly concerned about Allen's checkered past and leaped at the opportunity to have the No. 1 overall pick as an endorser.

"If we had hesitated, somebody else would have grabbed Allen," Reebok public relations director Dave Fogelson said back in 1996. "That's the way this business works.

"We looked at it this way. With the coaching Allen received from John Thompson and the Georgetown program, and with David Falk as his representative, we felt there were strong people surrounding him.

"Allen handles the (high school arrest) situation in an extremely mature manner. Not to downplay the incident—it was very serious—but it wasn't a factor in our discussions about going after Allen Iverson. He comes out of such a strong program (Georgetown), with its teaching and mentoring, that we believed it was something in the past."

Allen's signature shoe with Reebok was called "The Question," a direct link to Allen's nickname "The Answer."

Back in 1996 Reebok was struggling in the "Sneaker Wars" even though it had superstar center Shaquille O'Neal as a client. The company's position was lagging among twelve-to-seventeen-year-olds. Their ad campaigns weren't connecting, and that's where Allen came in. He wasn't much bigger than some of the kids Reebok wanted to attract, so they could identify with him a lot easier than 7–1, 315-pound Shaquille O'Neal.

Allen's game was fast and flashy and exciting. And he was also part of the hip-hop, Generation X culture, which was just emerging as a force in American life.

"This is something I've been waiting for all my life," Allen said of the Reebok marketing campaign that was built around him. "I had a lot of input.

"All along they told me they didn't want to make me up. They didn't want it to turn out to be something that I'm not. They wanted to let me be myself. They're just going to let me be me, whatever that is."

Whatever that "me" was, Reebok liked it.

"Allen Iverson has already paid for his investment," Reebok vice president John Borders said in an interview about Allen in 1996. "He's already earned every dime we've given him. We're a struggling company. We didn't connect with a young audience. That's where Allen helped us.

"We all wanted to listen to him and see what he thought about himself. We wanted to know what his connection would be to that consumer base. He's helped us focus a campaign."

Now, it was time to turn his attention to what happened on the basketball court.

9 | Now It's a Job

Allen Iverson had lived his dream and had become the No. 1 overall pick in the 1996 NBA Draft, but it didn't take long for this kid, who just loved to play basketball, to understand that in the NBA, hooping wasn't a game, it was big business.

"Allen brings a new winning attitude," Philadelphia 76ers team president Pat Croce said the night of the NBA Draft. "He's a fellow who wants to win. If you like our selection or not, at least the whole city is talking about the Sixers. It's great to be in Philly right now."

Great was not a word that had been associated with the Philadelphia 76ers for a long time.

The origins of the franchise dated back to the start of the National Basketball League as the Syracuse (N.Y.) Nationals. The club joined the NBA in 1949.

The City of Philadelphia had one of the NBA's charter franchises—the Warriors—when the league played its first season in 1946.

But in 1962 the Warriors relocated to the West Coast to become the San Francisco (now Golden State) Warriors.

The NBA-void in Philadelphia did not last long. In 1963 the Nationals moved to the City of Brotherly Love and were renamed the 76ers in honor of the signing of the Declaration of Independence.

Since that time the Sixers have had an outstanding history of success and superstar players. As the 1966–67 NBA Champions, they finished 68-13 and featured NBA All-Time Fifty Greatest Players Wilt Chamberlain, Billy Cunningham, and Hal Greer. Many considered that Sixers team the best in NBA history.

From the mid-1970s, when the Sixers purchased the contract of Hall of Famer Julius "Dr. J" Erving, through the mid-1980s, the Sixers were one of the glamour teams of the league, along with the Boston Celtics and Los Angeles Lakers.

With Erving, Moses Malone, Maurice Cheeks, Andrew Toney, and Bobby Jones, Philadelphia won the 1983 World Championship, sweeping the Lakers in four games in the finals. Then, after staying competitive with Charles Barkley leading the way, the Sixers collapsed after the 1991–92 season when Barkley forced a trade to the Phoenix Suns.

From the 1990–92 to 1995–96 seasons, the Sixers set a NBA record by having five consecutive seasons in which they won fewer games than the previous season. With flops like Christian Welp, Kenny Payne, Shawn Bradley, Sharone Wright, and B. J. Tyler, their drafting was like a Who's Who of first-round failures.

Once John Lucas was fired after going 18-64 in the

1995–96 season, the Sixers had their fifth coach in six seasons in Johnny Davis.

Even though the City of Philadelphia was down on the Sixers, hope had been revived with the drafting of Jerry Stackhouse, who like Michael Jordan, had attended the University of North Carolina. Added to this was the optimism generated by the opening of a brand-new arena—then came the drafting of Allen Iverson with the No. 1 overall pick in 1996.

"It's funny, but some people believe that it's all on the player, that he gets drafted, gets a contract, that he should be able to figure it out," said then Sixers general manager Brad Greenberg, who was in his first year on the job in 1996. "That's not the case. It's a nurturing process, and even more so as the players coming out of that draft get younger and younger.

"You can't make it happen overnight, but there are some things you can do that will speed up the process. What's the expression, 'Youth is wasted on the young'? Let's be honest, young people need guidance. They might be good players, but this is all new to them."

Unfortunately for Allen, he fell behind the eight ball right away.

To help rookies begin the adjustment to life in the NBA (not to mention their newfound status as millionaires), the league holds a mandatory rookie-orientation session.

Allen Iverson left the 1996 session in Orlando, Florida, one and a half days early and was fined $10,000 by the league.

"It was a mistake, and I handled it wrong," Allen said of

leaving the orientation. "I should have handled it better. I was sick, had food poisoning. I didn't mean any disrespect to the NBA."

Allen's on-court adjustment to the NBA was getting off to a similarly bumpy start.

The Sixers were not a good team, but at least every player had a defined role.

Second-year swingman Jerry Stackhouse had averaged 19.2 points as a rookie. Veteran forward Derrick Coleman had played only eleven games after being acquired the previous season, but he had always been good for 19 points and 10 rebounds. Small forward Clarence Weatherspoon hadn't lived up to the "Next Barkley" label he was given when the Sixers drafted him in 1992, but he had averaged about 17 points a game through his first four seasons. Center Michael Cage and reserves Don MacLean and Lucious Harris were all signed as free agents to help revitalize a team that had won just eighteen games in 1995–96.

Allen, as the point guard, was supposed to orchestrate things, distribute the ball, make sure everyone got his touch, keep everyone happy. But while he had a point guard's frame, it quickly became clear that Allen did not have a point guard's mentality.

Perhaps if the Sixers management would have listened a little more closely to some of the things Allen said days before the draft, they would have realized that.

"I'm going to play my game," Allen had said. "I don't think the Sixers would take me if they didn't want me to play my game.

"Philadelphia, if I go there, will be totally different than

Georgetown. Derrick Coleman, Jerry Stackhouse are both great scorers. I'll distribute the ball to them, but I'm definitely going to be looking for my shot.

"I don't know what a pure point guard is. I just play the game and do whatever is necessary to win. The Sixers are in a rebuilding phase, which is fine. It will take a little while for the other players to get used to me. But I don't plan on losing."

During six games in July in the Doral Arrowwood Summer League in New York, Allen's first opportunity to play for the Sixers, he averaged 29.5 points on 41.8 percent shooting. But as the Sixers' point guard, Allen averaged a team-high 22.3 shots a game and had 39 assists with 42 turnovers.

"Summer leagues are artificial settings," G. M. Greenberg said at that time. "What you see in those situations is very different compared to what goes on in the league. The games you see are not indicative of the league, of the league's style of play. For a player like Allen, the supporting cast is very different too."

Allen had said "it would be crazy" for people to think he would shoot like he did at Georgetown when playing with the Sixers, but through the team's first seven preseason games Allen went 38-for-96 from the floor.

"It's a good thing (Iverson's) got the green light to shoot," then Detroit Pistons coach Doug Collins said after a 1996 exhibition game with the Sixers in which Allen shot 6-for-17. "It looks like he's got the *neon* green light. He's lightning in a bottle. He plays like he did in college."

Johnny Davis had never been a head coach before, but he did play point guard in the NBA for a decade.

"I see some good things, but I see room for improvement," Davis said of his team and his young point guard. "Decision-making is something he will improve by gaining experience from playing more games.

"It's going to take time to define our personality, to learn what's expected, to play together. We're all experiencing growing pains. Once we come to the realization that we need each other, we'll start to make significant progress. Right now we're still trying to define who we are."

With Allen and Jerry Stackhouse as the centerpieces, the Sixers theme for the 1996-97 season was "The Revolution." And on November 2, 1996, Allen played in his first NBA regular season game.

The Philadelphia Flyers had already christened the CoreStates (now First Union) Center, but this was the first NBA regular season game to be played in the new arena.

A crowd of 20,444, the largest to ever see the Sixers play a home game, showed up for the opener against the Milwaukee Bucks.

Most of the eyes were on the Sixers' star rookie.

"I expect to win," Allen had said of his expectations for the upcoming season. "But it's going to take time for us to start winning. I think the attitude that Coach Davis has and the rest of the staff has is that they want to win. As long as the guys on the team understand that, we can get things done."

Clearly, Allen hadn't fully understood the implications of joining a team that had gone just 18-64 the season before. Allen had the first shot of his NBA career blocked and then shot two air balls, but he finished the night with 30 points and 6 assists.

Unfortunately, the Sixers lost 111–103.

"I thought we played together better tonight than we did in some preseason games," said Allen, who took a game-high 19 shots against the Bucks. "We can be and will be more effective together. We've still got eighty-one games to go. I'll definitely take every game as a learning experience."

Perhaps it was because the Sixers had been so awful for so long that fans had little patience. The team dropped their first three games, and the buzz in the city was that Allen was not a true point guard, and may never become one.

"He is a diamond who only needs a few of the rough edges knocked out," Sixers general manager Brad Greenberg said after Allen had taken a team-high 50 shots during the first three games. "He's doing extremely well. It's unfair to expect him to be everything in the first three games of his NBA career."

Although Allen led the team in shots, Jerry Stackhouse had taken 47 shots and Derrick Coleman 44. It wasn't a bad balance, but since Allen was the point guard, his high number of shots had him on the defensive.

"I honestly don't believe I'm a selfish player," Allen said. "People say that because I look to score and be the point guard. Ever since I was little, I looked to score. I just didn't grow tall enough to be a two-guard. But I'm also a creator.

"I haven't played the game I want to play yet. I want to be unstoppable in every fashion. Lots of steals, assists, points, and no turnovers. Just get into my grooves and don't look back."

Allen got that groove in the fourth game of the season when he scored 32 as the Sixers beat the Boston Celtics 115–105.

A victory over the Phoenix Suns followed, and then Allen was even more spectacular as he made his Madison Square Garden debut against the New York Knicks. Performing like a Broadway star, Allen dazzled the MSG crowd by scoring a then career-high 35 on 10-for-19 shooting. He had 5 three-pointers, 7 rebounds, 6 assists, and 2 steals as the Sixers stunned the Knicks 101–97.

"Everybody does a lot of talking before the game," Iverson said. "Once the game starts, it's no more talking. It's a show. Everything you've got, you got to show. All the other stuff, that just drives me harder. I'll make mistakes, but I'll do a lot of good things, too."

But there would be far more lowlights than highlights for the Sixers.

Allen was playing well, sometimes spectacularly. In fact, he would ultimately be named the NBA's Rookie of the Year after averaging 23.5 points, 7.5 assists, and 4.1 rebounds.

But the team as a whole was struggling.

During a 100–91 victory over the Orlando Magic on November 30, Coach Davis benched Allen after he committed his fifth turnover and then didn't hustle back on defense.

"It shocked me," Allen said of the benching. "It definitely shocked me. My man didn't score. I know my speed better than (Coach Davis) does. I got back. It wasn't like I wasn't playing defense.

"I got benched. Apparently, I wasn't producing. Apparently, it was a good decision to bench me because we came out with a victory. I don't have any problem with Coach Davis's decision."

Still, it was becoming apparent that Davis was over-matched as an NBA coach.

The team went into a tailspin, losing 23 of 24. By the All-Star Break, the Sixers were 12-34, and Coach Davis's job was in jeopardy.

"We are a work-in-progress," said G. M. Greenberg, who was also feeling the heat of the Sixers' poor start. "I'm disappointed but not discouraged. We are better than our record."

Consensus around the league was that the Sixers were too young in every area.

"Rebuilding takes time," a rival Atlantic Division general manager told a newspaper about the Sixers at the time. "When you throw together a mix of new ownership, a rookie coach, a rookie general manager, and a rookie point guard, then you have exponentially increased what can go wrong."

Allen was scoring more than 20 points a game, but he was shooting just 40 percent from the floor. He was averaging 7.1 assists and 4.7 turnovers, which was well below the 3-to-1 assist-to-turnover ratio top point guards have in the league.

"I'm still learning," Allen said. "I wish we had won more games. I think we were right there a lot of times."

But in his first four games after the All-Star Break, Allen shot a miserable 24.4 percent (19-for-78). Tiring of the questions about losing, Allen vowed not to talk to the media for the rest of the season.

"I don't see that it will hurt me or help me," said Allen, whose silence did not last that long. "I'm tired of saying things and then seeing what I said used a different way. I've already said everything I have to say."

Allen missed a practice in Miami and was benched for the start of a game against the Heat. It was the second time he had been benched at the start of a game for missing or showing up late for practice.

The house was crumbling.

An ill-fated meeting between President Pat Croce, Greenberg, and disgruntled season-ticket holders had Coach Davis backpedaling as the bandwagon calling for his job began to fill.

After the Sixers lost their fifth straight game, Coach Davis ripped into his team saying they were soft, did not demand respect from opponents, lacked confidence, and doubted one another.

"You can keep changing the guy in the hot seat, but at some point, you have to look down the whole bench," Coach Davis said while claiming he was not to blame. "It's always easier and cheaper to change the coach. But once you do that, you've still got the mirror standing there, and you've got to address the problem for what it is."

One problem, perhaps the biggest one, was the crumbling on-court chemistry between Allen and Jerry Stackhouse. Back in training camp, Allen and Jerry were talked about as potentially becoming the best young backcourt in the NBA.

"Every time I step on the court with Stack, I feel we can compete with any backcourt," Allen had said in October of 1996. "Everybody says we're too young, but that makes us work that much harder."

At the same time Stackhouse said, "There's nobody else

I'd rather be in the backcourt with. I think we can really make our mark. It doesn't have to be anything individual. I know we're young, but at some point we'll both be twenty-four, twenty-five, and have more experience."

Unfortunately, Allen and Jerry had to get through being twenty-one and twenty-two first, and that had become a struggle.

Stackhouse had seen his scoring average dip and his shooting percentage plummet. The whispers that Stackhouse and Iverson couldn't get along shouted onto the front pages of the newspapers when the two got into a late-season scuffle during a shoot-around.

"We're going to have spats," Stackhouse said of the incident. "We're family. What helps on the court a lot is our relationship off the court. That was an isolated incident. That's not something that's going to happen again."

Stackhouse had also questioned Coach Davis's preferential treatment of Allen. Of particular annoyance to him was when Coach Davis left Allen in the game during the closing seconds of a 131–110 loss to the Washington Bullets so he could score 40, and so become the first rookie to score 40 points in five straight games.

The Bullets let Allen have an open shot with 19.6 seconds left.

"The only thing we were trying to accomplish was Allen's pursuit of adding to the record," Coach Davis said. "That shot with 19.6 seconds left was his last crack at it."

It also became the last crack on the strained ego of Jerry Stackhouse. The day after the Washington game, Stackhouse exploded.

"I looked at it as if (the Bullets) were making fun of us," Stackhouse said of the gimme shot to Allen. "It was like 'Okay, we beat 'em, let 'em do what they want.' It was like it didn't really matter to them.

"My pride is big too. I'm a key part of this team. I like to have my touches. If I'm open, I want the ball, too. I don't say much, but when I say something, it's how I feel and what I mean. (From the point guard position) you can't shoot the ball that much at this level. You have to have other guys feed off you.

"Allen and I have talked. He understands how I feel, but it's not something that will just change overnight. Allen has made a lot of strides from the beginning to the end of the season. Allen is a scorer, and we understand that. But, like I said, in order for this team to be at its best and be able to compete with the best teams in the league, it's going to take everybody being involved."

Allen again reiterated that he was not a selfish player.

"I really don't think it's important about who scores or who does what," Allen said. "The most important thing is that we come out and play hard and try to win.

"People may not believe it, but I can go through a whole game and not score one point, but if we win the ballgame, I'm satisfied.

"The outline of this whole year has been that everything I try to do good, people make it negative. This talk that Jerry and I can't play together definitely falls into that category.

"I've got no problems with House, and I don't think he has any problems with me. Jerry and myself are going to be very successful in this league for a very long time."

Allen's first taste of individual success came when he was named NBA Rookie of the Year. In a ballot of 115 national media panelists, Allen received 44 first-place votes, nine more than Minnesota Timberwolves rookie point guard Stephon Marbury.

"In my heart, I knew who the Rookie of the Year was, but it wasn't up to me to decide," said Allen, who averaged 23.5 points, 40.1 minutes, 7.1 assists, and 2.07 steals.

But even in a moment of triumph, someone rained on Allen's parade. Boston Celtics Hall of Famer and Minnesota Timberwolves General Manager Kevin McHale said Stephon Marbury should have won because he helped his club win 40 games and reach the playoffs for the first time.

"I'm disappointed, I think the award went to the wrong guy," McHale said. "If they called the award the Most Valuable Rookie, Steph would've won it easy.

"(Allen Iverson winning) sends a bad message to these kids: 'Come in, jack it up, your team loses, but you're Rookie of the Year.' They should find someone who contributed to a winning team.

"Steph sacrificed his game for the betterment of his team. Iverson asked his teammates to sacrifice their game for his betterment."

Allen brushed McHale's criticism off the way he had with other criticism the entire season, but he couldn't help but feel hard done by.

"I think I got a bad shake this year," Allen said. "I got the short end of the stick. I don't feel that way right now, but this year was tough, man.

"After all the things I've been through in my life, where I come from, being incarcerated, coming up in a rough neighborhood, not even supposed to make it. I didn't feel people should've come at me like that.

"If someone was to go through what I've been through ... I would take my hat off to (them). It didn't seem like people wanted me to be successful. I read all the negative articles about me. It wasn't me. I'm not the guy those people made me out to be.

"I want people to know, if they can. If someone lied about something I said, I just want people to know they lied. It may reach some kid that looked up to me, and he'll find out that it's all right to follow what Allen Iverson is trying to do.

"There's a lot of kids that have been locked up, but now they know they can still do whatever they want to do to be successful. Somebody might read that, and that's good enough for me."

10 || Degeneration X

One of the biggest fallacies concerning Allen Iverson is that he came into the NBA as an authority-defying, hip-hop, counterculture, revolution-starting figure.

Allen certainly had some rough edges, and even he admitted he carried some baggage along, but what he really wanted was to be given a clean slate, to have a chance to let his present and future actions define who he was, not his past ones.

"All I want is for people to try to understand me," Allen said. "Just try to understand, you know, the way I am. It's better than just seeing something on TV, 'Oh, this guy's a terrible guy.' Or reading something in the paper. Sometimes that hurts and it bothers me because I know I'm not the bad person people make me out to be."

Those "people" would be the media.

It seemed that Allen had become a target for the national press from the night he was drafted first overall by the Philadelphia 76ers.

His background, his friends, his look, his style all became issues that quickly turned his image into that of an undisciplined Generation X basketball thug.

The irony is that when Allen first entered the league, he did not have his now signature cornrows. He wore a short afro with sides cut even shorter. He had yet to get many of the tattoos he now wears.

Yet the criticism rained down. It went like this: If it was associated with Allen Iverson, then it had to be bad.

"A lot of people judge Allen without knowing him," Sixers general manager Brad Greenberg said early during training camp in 1996. "You hear ESPN say the league is investigating Allen because of who his friends are, and it wasn't true.

"It *is* true that he has a lot of friends, but the two guys living with him are people he grew up with.

"He's a young guy going through some adjustments, the same type of adjustments anyone at the age of twenty-one would face. This is the first time he's living by himself, away from the structure of a college campus, away from a strong figure like (Georgetown coach) John Thompson.

"The good part is, he has a structure of a team again, the guidance of coaches, the comfort zone of being on the court where he flourishes."

Allen's friends—variously described as his "posse" or "The Hampton Mafia"—were thought to be bringing Allen down by pulling him into some kind of trouble. Many suggested that Allen should simply dump his lifelong companions.

Allen bristled at those suggestions.

"You know my friends have been with me before all

these people who are now writing stories about me even knew my name," Allen said. "When I was locked up in jail, those guys were with me. They came to see me, not the media people writing stories. Not these basketball players that think they know me. They don't know who I am, and want to criticize me.

"We're not a posse. I don't know why people say we're a posse, or that I have an entourage. Maybe the people who say that have no friends. Maybe they're mad at me because I have friends. Maybe they're scared of my friends. I don't understand, but it doesn't bother me."

Sixers' President Pat Croce once told Allen's friends that if they got Allen in trouble, he would burn their houses down.

"Yeah, I said it," Croce said, "but Allen knows how I am. It was nothing. I don't mind his friends. I've got friends who people would look at funny."

"People need to understand that he's intensely loyal," said Gary Moore, a longtime confident of Allen. "If you're a friend of Allen's, it stays that way for life. I don't care what you're doing or who you're with, he'll stand by your side because that's the way he is. . . . He won't change because of money or because of status. He'll only change if you prove to be something other than his friend, or if you're harming his family."

Allen's intense loyalty was again displayed the day after he received the 1996–97 Rookie of the Year Award. He went down to Hampton to testify on behalf of Michael Freeman, the man he calls father, who was convicted of drug dealing.

Despite his claims to the contrary, however, to many

NBA observers, fans and media, Allen was still just another young African-American thug from the ghetto who happened to be able to play basketball.

"I say to myself, I got locked up for a lot of people lying on me," Allen said. "The witnesses they had against me lied on the stand, and that was in the file, but I get locked up.

"Then I say to myself, I got off the whole thing, it was overturned. I should've never went to jail in the first place. But people still look at me as a bad person.

"I made mistakes in my life, and I'm going to continue to make them. But I feel like a mistake is only a mistake if you do it twice.

"I just don't want people to think I'm some bad guy. I'm not the bad boy of the NBA by far. But I've said it a billion times, there's gonna be a billion people who love Allen Iverson and a billion that hate him. I wanna do everything for the people that love him and be positive for the people who hate him."

But that was going to be hard to do when even many of Allen's NBA peers were criticizing him at every opportunity. This had much to do with the fact that in 1996 the NBA was going through a period of transition.

Established stars like Michael Jordan, Charles Barkley, Scottie Pippen, Karl Malone, David Robinson, John Stockton, and others were still around, but younger stars like Allen, Stephon Marbury, Kobe Bryant, Grant Hill, Shaquille O'Neal, and Kevin Garnett were stepping on to the scene.

Like many clashes of old versus new, "respect" was at the root of the friction.

In the second game of his NBA career, Allen had played

**College days—
Allen at
Georgetown.**

*Philadelphia Daily News/
George Reynolds*

**Allen's
trademark
drive to
the basket
came
early.**

*Philadelphia Daily News/
George Reynolds*

Allen's mother, Ann, revealing her loyalties.

Philadelphia Daily News/Yong Kim

No pain, no gain.

Philadelphia Daily News/ George Reynolds

How does he do it? Six-foot Allen scores over 6'11" Ervin Johnson of the Milwaukee Bucks.

Philadelphia Daily News/ George Reynolds

Allen celebrates as Toronto's Vince Carter misses a shot at the buzzer to send the Sixers to the 2001 NBA Finals.

Philadelphia Daily News/ George Reynolds

Sixers' coach Larry Brown accepts a hug from Allen;
Pat Croce, the team's president, shares the love.

Philadelphia Daily News/ G. W. Miller III

A
happy
man.

*Philadelphia
Daily News/
George
Reynolds*

Little big man— teammate Matt Geiger gives Allen a hug.

Philadelphia Daily News/ George Reynolds

Family man— with his daughter, Tiaura, and son, Deuce, after winning the 2001 Eastern Conference Finals.

Philadelphia Daily News/ Yong Kim

NBA commissioner David Stern presents Allen with his 2001 MVP award, making Ann Iverson as proud as can be.

Philadelphia Daily News/ George Reynolds

Deuce gets a kiss from Daddy.

Philadelphia Daily News/ George Reynolds

That's gotta hurt—Allen gets the full force of the Lakers' Shaquille O'Neal in Game One of the 2001 NBA Finals.

Philadelphia Daily News/ George Reynolds

Two superstars collide— Allen Iverson and the Lakers' Kobe Bryant, NBA Finals 2001.

Philadelphia Daily News/ George Reynolds

MVP

Philadelphia Daily News/G. W. Miller III

against Michael Jordan and the Chicago Bulls. It was a relatively uneventful game in which the Bulls blasted the Sixers, and Allen lived another lifelong dream of playing against Jordan.

"It was just wild," Allen said of playing against Michael Jordan for the first time. "I can't even remember the feeling. Just being on the court, playing against the greatest basketball player on the planet.

"I wasn't out there crazy in awe or anything like that because that's just not me. Once we get on the dance floor, I'm not going to be in awe of anybody. But it was a crazy feeling just playing against him."

But a few weeks later Chicago Bulls forward Dennis Rodman, who was notorious for his ill behavior, told some Chicago reporters that Allen had told Michael Jordan during the game that he didn't have to respect any other players.

Rodman, of all people, said Allen didn't respect the game and labeled him as the poster child for overhyped and overpaid players from the hip-hop, Generation X culture.

Rather than consider the source, the media ran with the story.

Suddenly Allen was known nationwide as the thug-rookie who had disrespected Michael Jordan.

The New York Post, however, reported that while Rodman and Bulls forward Scottie Pippen were criticizing Allen during a game, Michael Jordan approached Allen to tell him not to worry about it, and Allen responded by telling Michael Jordan, "Get the hell away from me!"

Allen, who grew up admiring Jordan as a player, wasn't going to stay silent about that.

"What? I'm going to tell Michael Jordan to get the hell away from me?" Allen queried. "They're trying to make me out to be another Rodman or something."

Allen admitted that he did tell Jordan that he was not going to respect him while they were on the court as opponents, but that his meaning got twisted.

"(Michael Jordan) said something about we are gonna respect him if we don't respect anybody else," Allen said. "I told him I wasn't gonna respect anybody. Not anybody that I am over here playing against.

"I respect everything that Michael Jordan has done for himself, everything he has done for his family, his friends, everything he has done for the city of Chicago. I respect all of that. But once you get on the court, I mean business. You've already lost the battle if you overrespect your opponent.

"What can I do (about the story)? It never happened, but what can I do?"

While Allen's argument made sense, it was not good enough for a number of NBA veterans—particularly former 76er Charles Barkley, who jumped into the fray and started referring to Allen as "Allen Me, Myself, and Iverson."

Barkley, who had been part of several notorious incidents including spitting on a little girl at courtside, said Allen should consider his teammates as his "posse."

As is his nature, Allen fired right back at Barkley.

"Charles Barkley needs to mind his business," Allen said. "I don't have an entourage. He'd never seen me with an entourage. All he knows about me is what he reads, what he hears. I don't go around spitting on people, or getting thrown out of games. I haven't done anything near what he has. Yet he's so perfect? All the negative things he's done?

"Even If I had an entourage, it wouldn't be near as bad as spitting on a little girl.

"What bothers me is that none of these guys tried to help me when I didn't have anything. I didn't hear anything positive from these people when I went to jail. They don't know anything about my life. I don't care what Charles Barkley does off the court. Why are they so worried about what I'm doing?"

It seemed as if everyone was coming down on Allen, including the NBA league office, which did a frame-by-frame analysis of his signature crossover dribble and deemed it illegal.

"It's just something to try and stop my progress, but it won't," Allen said. "From the beginning (the NBA) said my shorts were too long, my crossover is a carry. They questioned my friends. They said my ankle braces didn't permit enough white sock to show. I just take it on the chin and keep going."

Just before Christmas, *New York Post* NBA columnist Peter Vecsey reported that friends of Allen's and friends of his teammate Jerry Stackhouse's had gotten into an "impromptu rumble" outside the Sixers' practice facility.

Both players denied the incident happened, but it still made national news. Croce didn't mind the controversy that seemed to circle around Iverson. He also knew it would be viewed as a betrayal of trust if he tried to talk Allen into conforming to be what society wanted him to be.

"What some people do 'post-up,' Allen does 'alley-oop,' "

Croce reasoned. "And that's okay. I think that's what makes Allen special.

"But he understands his responsibilities. A lot of people don't realize how smart Allen is about life, both on and off the court. He knows the deal. He's a good person."

Still, the national perception of Allen was the opposite of Croce's, and the culmination of the anti-Iverson sentiment occurred at the 1997 NBA All-Star Game in Cleveland, Ohio.

It was also the celebration of the 50 Greatest Players in NBA History, and more than a few took their shots at Allen. The fact that the Sixers had lost 23 of 24 games made it much easier.

"Allen Iverson doesn't know anything," Charles Barkley said. "Grant Hill (of the Detroit Pistons) listened to us and took criticism. He didn't complain like Iverson. Do you think what a rookie says matters? It's all right to be an individual. Iverson can do what he wants. But there's no reason for a team that talented to lose 23 of 24. He should take criticism. (Veterans) have an obligation to be the caretakers."

"Iverson plays the game like a runaway train," Washington Bullets Hall of Fame forward Elvin Hayes said. "The bottom line is what your team does, and his team is not doing anything.

"If he doesn't show any respect for the (Top Fifty) and the top player of today, maybe he should read up on them. You'd expect more out of a kid like this who played at Georgetown under John Thompson."

By the time Allen was ready to play in the Rookie All-

Star Game, the sold-out crowd at Gund Arena had heard so many negative things about him that many of them actually booed him. They booed him during the introduction, the game, and when he was named MVP after he had 19 points and 9 assists.

"This isn't the first time I've been booed," said Allen, who for the first time wore the cornrows that would become part of his trademark. "I mean, it's natural to be booed at another team's home when you're playing them. But I didn't feel they were going to boo me during the rookie game.

"That's their opinion. That's not something I'm going to let bother me. It's not hard to deal with for me because there are so many other negative things that have happened in my life. It just helps me work that much harder to come into the stadium and hear some people boo me for going out and playing hard."

Allen was especially hurt that weekend by the number of veteran players who decided it was okay to bash him, even though most had never met him.

"I've had to deal with veterans coming at me and saying a lot of negative things," Allen said. "I would never downgrade another player. I know a lot of these players have their own opinion of me. If that's what they believe, then fine.

"There's no reason for (the veterans) to be against me. Whatever they say about me is their opinion, but it's not fair for someone who doesn't know me to say things. I'm not the person the media makes me out to be.

"Because you're a rookie, you just bow down? Not me.

I'd rather take the negative publicity. They say you have to pay your dues. I pay my dues on the court."

While Allen was having his issues with the media and the older players of the league, there was another segment of American society that was wholeheartedly embracing him.

Reebok put Allen's signature shoe "The Question" on sale on the Thursday before the All-Star Game. It sold out nationwide by Saturday.

"Allen's not viewed as negative by the kids," Reebok chairman Paul Fireman said back in 1996. "I don't think anybody should be against him. He's not a follower, and he's going to be himself. But that doesn't make him bad."

By now it was clear to everyone that Allen was a different kind of NBA star.

He had never said he wanted to be like Michael Jordan or Grant Hill. He never claimed to have a clean-cut, All-America image acceptable to all segments of society. As an example, Allen carried a registered handgun, which he said he needed "for protection."

"I'm disliked. The media has people out there thinking I'm some kind of bad guy. Some people might want to try me. I wear jewelry. People know I have money. Crazy things are occurring every day in this life. Bill Cosby's son (Ennis) was killed. I don't know if having a gun would've saved his life. People in this world are crazy. I just want to feel safe."

Allen never said he was anything other than who he was.

He was shaped by living in poverty in a drug-infested, gun-infested neighborhood. He was hardened by being tried and convicted of a crime he feels he didn't commit.

"I was eighteen, in jail," Allen said, in one of the most revealing commentaries of his rookie year. "I was seventeen, a minor, having to worry about newspapers writing negative things about me.

"My picture on the front page. I had to go to school in the summer to graduate from high school, then go right to college.

"I definitely started anew. I got another chance. The chance I almost had snatched away from me when I was sent to prison. I never should have gone to jail in the first place. But maybe if that wouldn't have happened, I wouldn't be in the NBA now. God has his ways.

"So if people have a negative feeling about me, and don't know me, so be it. I feel bad if people think I'm some kind of bad person. I'm not."

That was the way twenty-one-year-old Allen Iverson saw the world. A contract worth more than $9 million with the Sixers wasn't going to change who he was, and neither was a $40 million contract over ten years with Reebok.

This was Allen Iverson. Take him or leave him.

"I've represented some very conservative athletes, but I don't want Allen to be like them," Allen's agent David Falk said back in 1996. "I want him to be like he is.

"People complain about his hairstyle, his (hip-hop) lifestyle, but that's who he is. He shouldn't change.

"There's a great misperception of the person Allen is. Allen hasn't kicked anyone (like Dennis Rodman did), spat on anyone (like Charles Barkley did), missed a practice or anything.

"He's never going to be Grant Hill or Michael Jordan, and I don't want him to be. I want him to be Allen. When I was a kid my parents jumped on me for listening to the Beatles. Allen listens to something else. The next generation will listen to something else."

11

New School Meet Old School

Pat Croce knew he had made a mistake. He had rolled the dice while trying to remake his floundering ball club, and the Philadelphia 76ers team president had crapped out.

It wasn't just that the Sixers had finished a miserable 20-62. It was that the team clearly lacked the direction and guidance to move forward. So just a few days after the end of the 1996–97 season, Croce fired both first-year coach Johnny Davis and first-time general manager Brad Greenberg.

The Sixers clearly needed to make a big impact, and Croce knew just how to do it. He was going to lure Rick Pitino from the University of Kentucky to coach the Sixers.

"I'm going to get him," Croce said with his typical exuberance. "I'm going to get him."

Coach Pitino did end up leaving Kentucky, but it wasn't for the Sixers. He went to try and rebuild the most storied franchise in the NBA—the Boston Celtics. The Sixers had to settle for Croce's backup plan. It would turn out to be the best decision the franchise could have made.

On May 5, 1997, the Sixers introduced Larry Brown as the new head coach and vice president of basketball operations.

Coach Brown had a reputation as one of the best in the business, but he also had the reputation of being a vagabond.

"A long, long time," Brown said when asked how long he planned to be with the Sixers. "That's always been my goal, but I've never been ashamed of the job I've done or the effort I've put forth."

The Sixers' job was Brown's ninth stop in twenty-five years of coaching. His longest stint had been five years with the Denver Nuggets in the mid-1970s and five years at the University of Kansas, where he led the JayHawks to the 1987 NCAA Title.

But Coach Brown was successful at every stop. His specialty was reclamation projects, taking losers and quickly turning them into winners. He had only two losing seasons on his résumé.

Before Coach Brown arrived in Indiana in 1993, the Pacers had never won a playoff series. In his four-year tenure the Pacers averaged fifty victories and twice went to the Eastern Conference Finals.

Still, there was a catch.

"Larry is the ultimate fix-it man, but sometimes he gets on guys' nerves," said Ed Manning, who served as an assistant to Brown at Kansas and the San Antonio Spurs. "If he can't get it done, if he wants it done a certain way, and it just isn't happening—that really upsets him.

"I think (the Sixers) will see immediate results. Sure, Larry will piss off a lot of them, but they'll play better."

After a disappointing rookie season where he lost more games in one year than he had combined in high school and college, Allen said he was looking forward to playing for someone with more credentials than Coach Davis.

"The first thing we need is a strong coach, someone with a 'my way or the highway' attitude, someone willing to teach us," Allen said a few days before Coach Brown was hired. "We need someone we could have a relationship with besides on the court. I want to sometimes go into my coach's room and just hang out, someone who stresses defense, who knows the way he wants things run.

"Look at my stats, my (league-leading 337) turnovers. You can see I'm a rookie, that I have a lot to learn, a long way to go. I can't get there by myself."

Coach Brown was definitely the teacher Allen needed, but it remained to be seen whether or not Allen would be a willing student.

Things were certainly going to be different under Coach Brown. His title of vice president of basketball operations meant that he had final say in all basketball-related matters including the fact that Coach Brown had the power to trade any player—even Allen Iverson.

"When I've taken a job, if we won pretty quickly, they always say the previous guy couldn't coach or we had good players all along," Coach Brown said. "Then there was a reluctance to change and move forward.

"Our goal is to win a championship, not just get better. I want to have the ability to tell somebody these are the type of players I feel comfortable coaching, this is the style of play we need and we have to look for these type of people to fit in."

So if Brown thought that Jerry Stackhouse, whom he called a "great place to start," wasn't going to develop, he could trade him. If he thought underachieving Derrick Coleman, whom he called one of the league's "five best talents," became too much of a pain in the rear, he could trade him. And if he thought Allen, the NBA Rookie of the Year, who he said "has a will to win, which is something you can't teach," would never develop into a top-flight point guard, he could be sent packing too.

"No one is untouchable," Sixers' chairman Ed Snider said when Brown was hired. "We will do whatever we have to do to improve this team. If we have to take a step backward for a year, we will if it means we're taking a step forward for the long haul. The fans will show patience if they believe in what the organization is trying to do."

It seemed like the perfect marriage. Allen wanted a disciplinarian who knew all of the intricacies of basketball. And Coach Brown was certainly that.

But something wasn't right.

Larry Brown had been named coach of the Philadelphia 76ers on May 5. He had hired Billy King as his top lieutenant. He had engineered a huge draft-day trade that sent the rights to Keith Van Horn, the second overall pick in the draft, to the New Jersey Nets for the rights to Tim Thomas.

Coach Brown was more than two months into his program to rebuild the Sixers, but he had yet to meet face-to-face with Allen Iverson.

Allen had accepted his Rookie of the Year trophy in

Philadelphia on May 1 and literally hadn't been seen or heard from since.

Technically, Allen's on-court responsibilities to the Sixers didn't start until training camp opened in October, but it would figure that the team's new coach and star player would want to at least meet and have lunch together.

But it was late in July, and Allen and Coach Brown were still strangers. If there was tension between the two, the reasons for it weren't evident.

During Allen's rookie season, Coach Brown impressed Allen by greeting him during the Sixers game with the Indiana Pacers. And at the time of his hiring, Brown had said he was looking forward to coaching and getting to know Allen.

In June, Allen had gone to Brazil, Argentina, and Chile on a joint promotional tour between his shoe company Reebok and the NBA. But there had still been opportunities to make contact.

"I haven't spoken with Allen since I took over," Brown said.

But on July 22 rumors were floating around Philadelphia that Allen was going to be at Temple University's McGonigle Hall to play in an exhibition game featuring the Sixers' rookies and free agents and some local Philadelphia professionals.

"Allen was supposed to come (yesterday) morning (to the Sixers' rookie and free-agent practice)," Brown said before the game. "But he didn't. Then I heard he was coming to play tonight, so that's about it."

What followed was one of the more bizarre incidents in Sixers' history.

Allen did indeed show up for the game. He played 34 minutes, scored 21 points, had 7 assists, 5 rebounds, and 2 blocked shots.

All of this while Brown was sitting courtside, no more than fifteen feet from the action.

But despite both being in the same building, Allen and Coach Brown never spoke to each other. Allen chatted briefly with general manager Billy King after the game, but neither he nor Coach Brown made the effort to meet.

"Nah, nah, not with me," Coach Brown said when asked if there were any concerns that he and Allen had not met.

Allen's only response when asked about Coach Brown was "gotta go" as he headed out of the building.

Sixers President Pat Croce was just happy to see his star player.

"Oh, I think it's great that Allen showed up," he said. "I gave him a big hug when I saw him."

It wasn't until August 15 that Coach Brown and Allen finally had their first meeting.

"I had a great meeting with Allen," Brown said before returning to his home in Los Angeles. "All summer, he's been busy, and I've been busy.

"It seemed like the appropriate time since I was in Philly and he was in Philly. We sat down and kind of got to know each other and got acquainted."

But because of an incident that had occurred with Allen two weeks earlier, he and Coach Brown had much more to talk about than basketball.

12 | Trouble with the Law

For the better part of his rookie season, Allen had complained that people criticized him for no other reasons than they didn't like the way he looked, the friends he had, or the image he portrayed.

But on August 3, 1997, Allen gave his many critics something tangible on which to base their criticisms.

Early that morning in New Kent County, Virginia, about forty-five minutes from Allen's hometown of Hampton, he was arrested and charged with misdemeanor drug possession. According to Virginia state police spokesperson Mary Evans, Allen's 1996 Mercedes was pulled over on Interstate 64 at 1:27 A.M. after it was clocked going 93 mph in a 65-mph zone.

Inside the car with Allen were Maduro Earl Hill, thirty-two, of Hampton, and Damon Darnell Stewart, twenty-five, of Hampton.

Hill was the driver.

Spokeswoman Evans said that after pulling the car over,

state trooper Michael Pierce approached the car and "smelled the distinctive smell of marijuana" coming from Hill's open window. State trooper Pierce then asked the three men to step out of the car.

A search of the car revealed a .45-caliber pistol registered to Allen. Police said they also found a marijuana joint under the front passenger seat where Allen was sitting and a crumpled-up joint near Stewart in the backseat.

Allen was arrested and charged with misdemeanor drug possession. He had also originally been charged with possession of a firearm with a controlled substance, but that charge was dropped because it applied only if a pound or more of drugs were found with the weapon.

Stewart was also charged with marijuana possession, and Hill was charged with reckless driving.

All three were taken to the New Kent County jail. Allen was released on $2,000 bail.

"I didn't have the opportunity to speak to Allen yet, but it upsets me and disappoints me," Sixers President Pat Croce, one of Allen's biggest supporters, said during a hastily called press conference. "With all the hard work we have done on and off the court to get this turned around to a positive tilt, this taints it.

"As a fan, a father, and a Philadelphian, it bothers me, disappoints me, and upsets me whenever you have one of our athletes breaking the law. Allen is a role model. Whether they were his joints or not, he was in a situation of being in a car with marijuana. I don't want kids looking at him and thinking it's cool to smoke joints."

Coach Brown, who still hadn't met with Allen since

being hired, joined in on the conference-call from his home in California.

"When you sign a contract to play in this league, you've got to be responsible. Kids look up to you, and you're representing not only yourself but a lot of other people, Philadelphia and the 76ers," Coach Brown said. "You can't do stuff like this. It's not acceptable for anybody, much less a guy who's a public figure and representing so any people.

"I'm not concerned with coaching Allen Iverson right now. I'm more concerned with his image and that of the 76ers. Maybe this will be a great lesson for him. Maybe he'll start to realize he has to be responsible."

For Allen, all the skeletons were being dragged out of the closet again—his earlier arrest, his questionable friends, his thug image. The feeding frenzy had begun, and Allen's critics were hungry for more to chew on.

Later Allen would say that the incident was the result of his poor judgment.

"That was so stupid," Allen would say. "It was such poor judgment. I let this guy I'd never been with drive my car.

"I mean, I don't know what the guy has on him. I don't even know if he knows how to drive a Benz. I just try and learn from every experience in my life. Everything that goes on in my life, I try to learn from. I make mistakes. I think I'll make more mistakes in my life. I'm just praying that it's not with the law."

Because Allen's 1993 maiming-by-mob conviction had been overturned, Linwood Gregory, the district attorney overseeing the case in New Kent County, said Allen would be prosecuted as a first-time offender.

The maximum penalty Allen faced was a year in prison and a $2,500 fine.

On August 27, 1997, Allen appeared in the New Kent County General District Court and pleaded no contest to a concealed weapons charge. In making this particular plea, Allen avoided prosecution on the misdemeanor marijuana possession charge. Under the agreement, Allen acknowledged that there was sufficient evidence to find him guilty of unlawfully carrying a concealed weapon.

In return, Gregory agreed not to prosecute the drug charge.

As a result, Allen was placed on three years' probation. He was also required to undergo a monthly drug test for two years and was not allowed to own a gun for two years. Allen was also required to perform 100 hours of community service.

It was clear to all that Allen was determined not to have the possibility of a drug charge on his record. He always denied the marijuana found under the seat was his. The probation agreement he accepted was three times more severe than what he would've faced had he been convicted of the misdemeanor drug charge.

On the Sixers Media Day in October, Allen did not shirk away from his responsibilities during his hectic summer. He again said he was embarrassed by what had happened.

"It's something I wish would have never happened," Allen said. "The only thing I can do is move forward. Since I was seventeen and got into the incident I was in (the bowling alley brawl), I've wanted to turn over a new leaf and be a better person in society.

"It's unfortunate that this latest incident happened. I didn't want it to happen to me, but I made a mistake. It's something I'll continue to learn from."

While many initially tried to link Allen's trouble to his friends, he said the people he was arrested with were business associates, with whom he was discussing a record deal.

"I can't put this on my friends and say this happened because of them, because I wasn't with my friends," Allen said. "I wasn't with people who I call my friends. That was the mistake I made. I just want to be smarter with everything I do from now on."

On the plus side, his shoe company Reebok International said they had no plans to sever ties with Allen.

"We said at the outset we were standing by Allen," Reebok public relations director David Fogelson said right after Allen's plea agreement. "I don't think the judge's decision would have any impact on our association with Allen.

"What's important is integrity and perseverance. Allen has persevered to get to where he is. He's forthright and has integrity.

In fact, on October 28, 1997, Reebok launched Allen's second shoe called "The Answer" by adorning three Amtrak trains with the Reebok logo and sent them from Philadelphia to New York. The one-day launch cost Reebok $150,000, and the company committed $10 million to promoting the shoe. Allen's first shoe, The Question, had sold more than 250,000 units.

But everyone was not as forgiving as Reebok. In September Allen had been called to New York to meet with NBA commissioner David Stern.

"He came at me like he was supposed to, very strict," Allen said of Commissioner Stern. "I didn't expect him to come in there, smile in my face and say I was doing great things and what happened can continue and doesn't matter.

"When people look up to me like they do, I can't be in the media for what I was in for this summer. I would have accepted any type of punishment he gave me because I deserved it."

On the first day of training camp, the league announced that it had suspended Allen without pay for the Sixers' season opener.

"This is going to hurt," said Allen, who lost $38,154 in salary for the suspension. "It's something I didn't expect. I wish I had known a lot sooner, but it's a decision they made and I respect it and have to live with it. It's going to hurt to miss one game, but I have eighty-one more, that's the way I have to look at it.

"I'm just glad I can put the summer behind. I'm glad to get started again and do what I love to do."

13 | A Clashing of Styles

The addition of veteran coach Larry Brown had given the Sixers hope that the 1997–98 season would be one of great progress.

Allen and Coach Brown hadn't got off to a great start as they took more than two months to meet. And when they did, it was under the cloud of Allen having been arrested for misdemeanor marijuana possession.

But by the time the Sixers opened training camp at the University of North Carolina—Coach Brown's alma mater—Allen's legal problems had been resolved. And while the NBA had suspended him for the first game of the regular season, it was basically back to basketball for Allen.

There was no doubt that his star guard was the primary thing on Coach Brown's mind.

"I want Allen to be the best guard in the league, and he has a chance to be," Coach Brown said the day before the start of training camp. "He wants to win the game. Last year he looked around, there were a lot of guys he didn't feel were trying to win the game.

"I don't fault that. I think Allen will do what we want. I don't want to take away his individual skills. . . . But it's tough when a point guard takes the ball down court and shoots it because he has the ability to beat somebody and the other four guys never touch it."

Still, despite his praise of Allen's talents, Coach Brown was clearly concerned about Allen's ability to become an NBA point guard in the classic mold.

In June the Sixers had considered drafting University of Colorado point guard Chauncey Billups so as to give Allen more time off the ball.

But the Sixers eventually shipped the rights to Utah All-America forward Keith Van Horn to the New Jersey Nets in an eight-player deal that got the Sixers rookie forward Tim Thomas and veteran guard Jim Jackson.

"I look at (Detroit Pistons Hall of Famer) Isiah Thomas coming into the league," Coach Brown said, making a comparison to Allen. "He was wild as a hare, but had the same kind of drive that I see in Allen.

"This kid, I've never seen stuff like him. He wants to win so bad. He's so skilled. He gets to places so fast, has so much pride. Sometimes he thinks he has to do it himself. But as an old coach of mine said, guys who don't make mistakes never do anything to help their team."

Allen knew that Coach Brown, as a former All-America point guard at the University of North Carolina, understood the position but that he also had a reputation of being hard on his point guards.

Still, Allen embraced the opportunity to play for Coach Brown.

"I think God sent me Larry Brown," Allen said during training camp. "He's what we need. Of all the coaches available, he was the best coach for me.

"You hear people say he's too hard on point guards, that we wouldn't mix. None of that's true. Coach tells me what he wants, I go and try."

Allen took offense to the assessments that he had shot the ball too much during his rookie season. And that he was hard to coach.

"Ask (Georgetown coach John Thompson), ask Johnny Davis whether I was coachable," Allen said. "I did what Johnny wanted. Some games we were nine deep, and Coach Davis would tell me to score as much as I can.

"We have great talent, but this league is all about the coach. You've got to have a captain, a leader, somebody pushing, getting every little bit of talent out of you.

"Coach jumps on everybody, jumps on me, it's better for the team."

Allen, who was named as team captain during training camp, said he was committed to playing the Larry Brown way, and because of his new teammates, it would make it easier for him to distribute the ball.

"You saw the team we had last year," Allen said. "Who was going to score? I'd throw a pass, somebody would miss, the next time I'd say I'd rather do it myself. That's not the right way. You have to go to the guy again. People said I was trying to win the Rookie of the Year, but I was trying to win games.

"With the talent we have, with a strong-minded coach, I've got so much backup I don't have to score 40 or 50. I can score 10 and we can still win."

On paper the Sixers were better, but the team that Coach Brown opened the season with still had issues to resolve.

Allen was just a second-year player. Third-year guard Jerry Stackhouse was coming off a subpar sophomore season in which he had to play second fiddle to Allen. Tim Thomas had played just one season of college at Villanova, and Jim Jackson was on his third team in less than a year. Unreliable forward Derrick Coleman came to camp demanding to be traded, and hardworking small forward Clarence Weatherspoon was upset that he was back after a trade to the Boston Celtics fell through when center Dino Radja failed a physical.

The optimism Allen felt quickly faded as the Sixers started the 1997–98 season at 0-5.

Coach Brown was already frustrated and let everyone know it.

"We're not a team," he said after the Sixers lost 112–105 to the Seattle SuperSonics. "As soon as things go bad, we start playing like a bunch of strangers. We look like a summer league all-star game on MTV.

"How can you call us a team when we won eighteen and twenty-two games the past two seasons? That ain't a team. We don't play like a team. A team does little things . . . they get on the floor for loose balls, they block out, make an extra pass, set a screen."

Allen was taking the losing hard. As the point guard and

star player he was the focal point of the team. Coach Brown was riding him hard.

"For the first time in my life, I wasn't having a good time playing basketball," Allen said sixteen games into the season. "Even last season, with the bunch of losses, I had a whole lot of fun just being out on the court, playing in the NBA.

"These first fifteen games weren't fun for me at all. The losing again was getting to me. But I wasn't playing my style either. I was letting other things bother me instead of going out there and just doing the things I love to do."

On December 14, a day after he had just two assists in a game against the New York Knicks, Allen missed a practice. Coach Brown sat Allen out of the next game against the Boston Celtics.

"I didn't want to keep anybody on the bench," Coach Brown said. "(Allen) caused that. That's the first time I've ever had to do it. It's not a pleasant thing."

The next day Allen apologized to his teammates and told the media that "Coach Brown didn't show any favoritism or anything. I made a mistake. I was punished for it. I think it was fair not letting me play."

Still, the Sixers were 6-15 and the seeds of tension between Allen and Coach Brown were starting to grow.

"I don't think Allen ever wants to do anything the wrong way," Coach Brown said. "He should be a senior in college. He's a young kid. I haven't been around anybody in my life who hasn't made a mistake once in a while."

By the middle of December, Coach Brown had seen enough to realize that his current mixture of players was not going to work.

Trade rumors had been circulating the entire year, and one said that the Sixers were going to trade Allen to Toronto for Raptors point guard Damon Stoudamire. Instead, on December 18, the Sixers made their first huge move in reshaping the roster. They traded Jerry Stackhouse and reserve center Eric Montross to the Detroit Pistons for 6-foot-10 shot-blocking center-forward Theo Ratliff and 6-5 guard Aaron McKie, a Philadelphia native who had played collegiately at Temple University.

"In the time we had Jerry here, we won eighteen and twenty-two games and were 6-16 this season," Coach Brown said. "Jerry's not the problem, but we had to make a change.

"It wasn't working on the court. I was hopeful Jerry and Allen could get together, but after I watched us play as a team, I didn't think it was going to work."

Allen didn't endorse the trade but neither did he pan it.

"This is going to be better for Stack," Allen said. "He'll fit better in Detroit. At times we worked well together. At times we didn't. We were starting to grow on each other, but things happen in life."

Stackhouse welcomed the trade, and as he left Philadelphia he made a prophetic comment that everyone would eventually come to realize.

"Iverson's a two guard, not really a point guard," he said. "He said it himself. He likes to put the ball in the basket. Well, that's my job."

Not everything was so bad. On January 18, 1998, Allen outdueled Michael Jordan by scoring 31 with six assists and three steals as the Sixers beat the Chicago Bulls for the first time in five seasons, 106–96, in front of 21,000 fans at the CoreStates Center.

"When I got here, I told everyone we were going to get better, we were going to play the right way," Coach Brown said. "It didn't happen as quickly as I had hoped. Now I see people caring about each other."

On January 18 Coach Brown made what looked like a minor trade at the time, but acquiring backup point guard Eric Snow from the Seattle SuperSonics for a second-round draft pick would ultimately have a dramatic affect on the Sixers and Allen.

Allen was finding his groove. During the second week of January, he averaged 25.3 points and 7.6 assists to earn Player of the Week honors.

Other players were noticing his improved play.

"Allen, that boy is something else," Miami Heat center Alonzo Mourning said after a late January game. "There's a difference in Allen—a complete difference. He's really turned himself into not just a scoring guard, but a guard that's controlling his team, making great decisions, distributing the ball, plus he's still scoring.

"He's utilizing the fact that he's a triple threat. I compliment him tremendously because of his work ethic and how he's growing."

Still, things weren't perfect. At the midway point of the season, the Sixers were a lowly 14-27.

Allen was averaging 20.6 points, 6.8 assists, and 2.6 steals. He felt his numbers were good enough to make the All-Star Game in New York, but he was not selected for the team.

"I felt like I should be playing with the best players in the league," Allen said of his All-Star snub. "I feel I am one of the best players in the league, but you've got to look at our record. If that's the reason why I wasn't selected, I can respect that. I hope to have a long career, and I'll be able to make the All-Star Game one day."

Despite his improved play, the relationship between Allen and Coach Brown was still uneasy. Coach Brown was a perfectionist, and Allen wasn't yet perfect. Allen said he didn't mind criticism, but he was getting increasingly annoyed that Coach Brown often chose to criticize his play in the media. The All-Star break provided another bump in the relationship when rumors circulated that the Sixers were trying to trade Allen to the Orlando Magic for All-Star guard Anfernee "Penny" Hardaway.

Coach Brown denied the rumor saying "All I know is (Orlando) called us and mentioned that they had some interest in our players. (General manager) Billy King said we had some interest in theirs, and Penny's name came up. But that was as far as it went. I see what it would take."

Allen and Coach Brown had a closed-door meeting to air the situation out.

"If you hear your name in trade rumors, it's not always bad," Allen said. "It's never bad because it means somebody wants you."

Allen also delivered a cryptic note to the media about his meeting with Coach Brown.

"It's something we've had before," he said. "That's a family thing. Maybe he'll be talking to you about what we talked about, but I wouldn't."

Then, on February 11, with the Sixers being blown out by the lowly Dallas Mavericks 85–71 with 5 minutes, 43 seconds left in the game Coach Brown made a minor adjustment in the lineup that would ultimately prove to be an epiphany.

Newly acquired Eric Snow went to the point, and Brown shifted Allen over to the two guard. With Allen free of play-creating responsibilities, he scored 12 points, including a three-pointer with 5.5 seconds left as the Sixers rallied to a 91–90 victory.

'You know I want to be out there doing my thing, getting up and down the court, penetrating, going to the rack," Allen said. "But in this league, you can take away from a lot of guys' talents and their ability too if you play like that all the time. That's why coach is trying to make me a point guard instead of an undersized two guard."

The trade deadline came and went, and the Sixers kept Allen. They did, however, trade Jim Jackson, Clarence Weatherspoon, and Terry Cummings to the Golden State Warriors for forward Joe Smith, Allen's AAU teammate from Hampton who had been the first overall pick in the 1995 draft.

Allen and Coach Brown's differing philosophies on how he should play were becoming more visible.

"Allen's such a tremendous talent that it's difficult to coach," said former NBA guard Glen "Doc" Rivers, who is now the coach of the Orlando Magic. "It's a two-steps-forward, one-step-backward process.

"It's tough to tell a guy to pass if he knows he can score. That's not a knock. Allen sees his game one way, his coach sees it another way. At some point there's going to be a meeting and it's going to work."

By this point, though, Allen had had enough.

For the entire season he had been trying to do what Coach Brown wanted him to do. He knew he was still learning and making mistakes and that Coach Brown wasn't always satisfied with his play, but he was tired of being criticized in the media.

Allen was in the second year of his three-year rookie contract, and during the summer the Sixers would have exclusive negotiating rights to try and sign him to a long-term extension.

But it would be Allen's final call, and he let Coach Brown know in no uncertain terms that he was frustrated with him too.

"I'll remember everything this summer," Allen said, referring to his upcoming negotiations. "I really will think about all the things that have been said about me this year."

Allen, who reads everything concerning him, was particularly annoyed by a comment Coach Brown made in a *Sports Illustrated* article when he said, "The company Allen's with is Reebok," not the Sixers.

"(Coach Brown) doesn't even know me off the basketball court to be able to say that," Allen said. "I think I have a good relationship with my teammates. I don't appreciate some of the things he says about me, but that's just the way it is with him.

"He's a great, great coach, but sometimes I feel he should talk to me in private. Sometimes I feel that he makes mistakes, too, but I wouldn't go into detail with the media about it. And I wouldn't say anything bad about him publicly."

Coach Brown wasn't backing down.

"My priority with Allen is to try and teach him the right way to play everyday," he said. "I think I would be doing him a disservice if I'm worried about how he's going to feel about me.

"I've said this all along, 'If you're supposed to be a great player, no matter what it takes, you do it.' He tells me all the time that he's the best point guard in the league. Then he has to go out every night and try to perform to that level."

On the face of it, the differences between Coach Brown and Allen Iverson couldn't be bigger. One is a twenty-six-year-old African-American kid from the streets of Hampton. The other is a sixty-year-old Jewish kid from Brooklyn. But in many ways they have more similarities in their personalities than differences. Both are emotional. Both are stubborn. Both say exactly what's on their mind. And neither is ever going to back down.

By the end of the 1997–98 season, Coach Brown and Allen had just about survived each other. The Sixers 31-51 record wasn't great, but it was the franchise's best since the 1991–92 season.

As Allen put it, "I know (Coach Brown) is a good coach. He's proven he's a good coach. Whether he's the best coach for me, I don't know." Now, with a summer of negotiations to come, it remained to be seen just where their relationship might end up.

"I don't have a problem with (Coach Brown). God did send him to me, just like I said. This is my team. This is my home. This is where I want to be. This is where I want to play."

14 | A Season of Firsts

As it had done in each of the previous seven years, the 1998–99 season for the Philadelphia 76ers began with hope on Draft Night.

In 1996, Allen Iverson was selected first overall, and in 1997 small forward Tim Thomas came in a draft-day deal.

During the previous season, the Sixers had traded guard Jerry Stackhouse, the third overall pick in 1995, to the Detroit Pistons for center Theo Ratliff and guard Aaron McKie, but Coach Larry Brown liked the makeup of the young team he was putting together.

With the eighth overall pick in the 1998 draft, the Sixers selected St. Louis University freshman guard Larry Hughes.

The idea was that Hughes, the 6-foot-5 consensus National Freshman of the Year, would team with Allen to become that dynamic young backcourt that Allen and Jerry Stackhouse could not.

"I was hoping weeks ago that our choice would be

Hughes," said Coach Brown, who for the second consecutive year drafted a player with just one year of collegiate experience. "And that's without slighting any of the other (top picks).

"When I look at our team and Allen and the way we'd like to play, you've got a 6-5 nineteen-year-old who I think can be a great ball handler and play both positions for us. I don't worry about 'one' and 'twos.' I'd like to have two guards who can handle the ball."

Allen also recognized the possibilities.

"I knew that Larry wanted to be here, and I wanted Larry to be here," Allen said on draft night. "Larry has a lot of talent for a nineteen-year-old. I'm twenty-three, so we can grow together.

"If he pays attention to Coach Brown, he'll be fine. I see he can handle the ball, so I can play some off guard and he can play the point. I'd still be the point guard. I still want to run the team. We're basketball players. We should be able to mesh."

Perhaps if it had been a normal summer, things would have worked out better.

Salaries for NBA stars had been escalating at an alarming rate. Players like Miami Heat center Alonzo Mourning, Minnesota Timberwolves forward Kevin Garnett, and Washington Bullets forward Juwan Howard had signed contracts for more than $100 million.

The collective bargaining agreement had expired and the owners, concerned that the players were getting too large a percentage of the revenues, tried to institute a salary cap that would curb the upward spiral.

The NBA Players Association balked at the idea, and a hostile labor impasse ensued. The owners instituted a lockout shortly after the draft and shut down all business operations. Teams weren't allowed to conduct business until the owners and players reached a new agreement.

Both sides dug in for a long, hard fight.

Allen had just finished the second year of his three-year rookie contract. He was in line to negotiate a long-term deal with the Sixers that would have surely put him in the $100 million category or make him a free agent after the 1998–99 season.

But with the lockout in place, Allen would have to wait. And since the Sixers could not conduct any basketball-related business, Larry Hughes would miss out on the rookie training camp and summer league.

While many of the league's high-profile players were attending union meetings, Allen stayed at home in Hampton.

On July 13, Allen again made negative headlines—not for anything he had done but because of those around him.

It should've been a fun time. Allen was hosting the 1998 Allen Iverson Celebrity Summer Classic—a full weekend of festivities designed to raise funds for the Boys and Girls Clubs of Greater Hampton Roads and the American Heart Association.

But hours before the kickoff, two of Allen's friends— Andre Steele and Michael Powell—were driving his $138,000 Mercedes when they were arrested in Norfolk, Virginia, on drug charges. According to Norfolk police, Powell was charged with felony possession of cocaine with intent to distribute. Steele was charged with possession of marijuana.

Allen was not involved in the crime in any way, nor was he brought in for questioning. That was crucial because Allen was still under three years' probation for his plea agreement on concealed weapons charges.

It was just more negative publicity that Allen didn't need.

"I don't think I learned that much from it, but I think my best friend (Andre Steele) did," Allen said. "He was always the one, when we were getting out of line, who calmed everything down, told us we can't do this, we can't do that. For him to get in trouble just took a toll. Everyone looked up to him as the perfect one, the one who did everything the right way."

The lockout continued into the fall and canceled the start of the regular season. On October 22, the players scheduled a union meeting in Las Vegas, and Allen finally said he was ready to get involved.

"It's my future, this is what I do," Allen said. "There was chaos going on in my everyday job, and I wasn't getting involved. I'm kind of disappointed in myself. It's another mistake I think I've made, waiting so long to get involved."

Off the court, Reebok introduced Allen's third shoe — The Answer II.

"Other guys aren't in the situation I'm in," Allen said. "I have a big shoe deal, some guys don't. I don't really know how long I can go without playing. I feel I can go a year, a whole season. I know others wouldn't be able to. I didn't think the lockout would last this long, be this serious. I didn't take it as seriously as I should have."

The lockout didn't last the whole season, but it did cost Philadelphia the 1999 All-Star Game. As a rising star and a Sixer, Allen might well have made his first All-Star team, but it was not to be.

On January 7, 1999, the owners and players came to an agreement. The league would play a fifty-game schedule beginning on February 5.

Under the new salary scale Allen would not be able to sign a $100 million contract, but he was satisfied with the maximum six-year, $70.9 million contract the new agreement allowed him to sign with the Sixers.

"The money that they have out there is enough for me to live off of," Allen said. "All I want to do is take care of my family. I'm not greedy. I don't have to make $20 million a year to play basketball, to do something I really love."

There were other changes too. Shortly after signing the contract, Allen fired his long-time agent David Falk, who had taken on his rival Stephon Marbury as a client and engineered his trade from the Minnesota Timberwolves to the New Jersey Nets.

Troublesome forward Derrick Coleman was bought out of his contract and Joe Smith was not re-signed. The Sixers spent big money on free agent center Matt Geiger, who had played the year before with the Charlotte Hornets.

They also signed shot-blocking center-forward Theo Ratliff to a long-term contract.

But before the season began, the NBA faced the retirement of Chicago Bulls' superstar Michael Jordan on January 13.

"I played against him, but at night I waited for the highlights to see what he did," Allen said. "I enjoyed watching him play. I enjoyed playing against him. It was a great experience playing against the world champions, a guy like that. Nothing can top that.

"He set the standard for everybody. I don't know if people can reach what he has done, but it is a challenge to try to get there. The greatest player in the game is leaving. I always thought I'd have a chance to state my case as one of the best. I didn't want him to leave this early."

The abbreviated training camp set in motion a chain of events. Coach Brown did not feel comfortable with rookie Larry Hughes beginning the season as a starter, so he decided to go with Eric Snow.

"I just want to take some of the pressure off the younger guys, not have them playing against the studs early," Coach Brown said.

Snow was a pure point guard, which meant Allen, at barely six feet, was going to play the shooting guard.

"Allen's a great scorer," Snow said. "It's no secret that he has a scorer's mentality. When I'm out there, he's told me his eyes light up because he knows I'm going to try and get him great shots. He's so great in transition, so hard to guard.

"In that situation, he has no point-guard responsibilities. It takes a load off him."

Allen was still calling himself a point guard, but a transition had begun.

Allen shot just 4-for-17, but the Sixers beat the Charlotte Hornets 78–66 to give Allen his first Opening-Day victory.

"Everybody can't have a great night every night," said Sixers guard Aaron McKie, who had become Allen's best friend on the team. "I told Allen, 'Would you rather have 40 points and a loss or 15 points and a win?' You choose. That'll show what type of player you are."

Allen was missing his shooting touch, but the Sixers jumped out to a 4-1 start. They also were displaying a new identity—that of a tough-minded defensive team.

Coach Brown was also pleased with the intensity and dedication to detail, particularly on the defensive end. Even when a four-game losing streak left the players scratching their heads at their 4-5 record, Coach Brown was satisfied.

"This is the proudest I've been in a long, long time," Brown said after a 76–69 loss to Atlanta. "It was as good a defensive period as we've played."

Allen, though, was itching to break out. He went on a ten-game tear during which he averaged 32 points, and finished February averaging 28.5 points, which was almost a third of the team's points, 6.0 assists, 5.8 rebounds, and 2.31 steals.

Allen joined Julius Erving, Moses Malone, and Charles Barkley as the only Sixers to be named NBA Player of the Month.

"I think I'm the best guard in the league," Allen said confidently. "I might not be, but I'm not going to say anybody is better than me. I worked hard to get here. I'm not going to say any guard is more talented than I am, and that's not being bigheaded or conceited. That's just confidence. But I know I have long way to go."

The Sixers were following their leader. They were off to a 9-5 start.

"We feed off the little guy," Aaron McKie said. "I've said from day one, there are no egos on this team. We have one superstar, and we know it. A lot of teams have three or four, and it doesn't work. We feed off of Allen, off his energy.

"I've seen Michael Jordan score, and no disrespect to Mike, but there are times when I sit there and say Allen might be the best I've ever seen at putting it in the basket for his size."

Allen was thriving at the off guard. Snow was running the offense and playing tremendous defense. The duo was clicking.

"When Allen gets to open spots, I see him," the Sixers true point guard Eric Snow said. "And there are times in games when you can sense the opponent's defense is slipping. If they're slow to react to Allen, it's too late.

"One thing about Allen is, he just wants the ball, to win. I mean, how many guys could start the season shooting 15-for-55 and come on the way he has?"

Everything was going well. Allen was playing better than he had at anytime during his career, and the Sixers were winning. Their 11-8 start was the best since the 1990–91 season. The only controversy was when Coach Brown traded a struggling Tim Thomas and center Scott Williams to the Milwaukee Bucks for veteran power forward Tyrone Hill, who added to the Sixers' toughness.

Then Allen messed up.

On March 11, 1999, Allen missed practice. He said that his girlfriend, Tawanna Turner, had recently had a miscarriage and was feeling unwell.

"My girl was sick," Allen said. "We've got kids, and I had to handle that. I'll handle any repercussions.

"They're talking about fining or suspending me. I called when it happened. I was on my way out the door."

Allen's bodyguard Terry Royster had called the Sixers, but that didn't satisfy Coach Brown, who also said it was "not the first time" Allen had missed practice.

"You should read our team rules," he said. "If this was one isolated incident, no problem. I've got a problem with this. It's a pattern. The rule is that if you have a personal problem, you call the coach. You, not someone else."

Allen was upset at Coach Brown. Once again he felt family business had been publicly aired. He was also upset that some of his teammates had spoken against him without identifying themselves.

Someone suggested that Allen was hanging out late with the rapper Mase, who was in town.

The next day the Sixers players held a forty-minute closed-door meeting.

First the players decided that Allen would not be suspended for missing practice, and second, they decided to bar the media from practices and shootarounds for the remainder of the season.

Never one to hide his feeling, Allen fired back to defend himself.

"I don't like some things that were said by (Coach Brown) and by my teammates, and they didn't say their names," said Allen, who scored 28 in the next game against the New Jersey Nets. "I addressed that. That was disgusting to me. I thought my professional family was a lot tighter than that.

"My reason (for missing practice) should have been enough. I'd do it the same way again. Ever since Coach Brown has got here, Terry has been the one to call. This is nothing new. Then out of the blue, that's not good enough?

"I guess people felt one of my friends (Mase) was in town, I was hanging out all night. I hang out all night anyway, if I want to. But I still come in here and give these people the same thing I always give them."

In the face of this conflict, the Sixers began to struggle. They finished March by losing three straight and five of six, but center Matt Geiger scored 25 and Allen added 24 points as the Sixers shocked the Heat 88–84 in Miami to improve to 16-14.

But Coach Brown and Allen had another flare-up the next night.

After going 0-for-7 in the first quarter of a game against Cleveland, Allen didn't start the second quarter. Then, with about two and a half minutes left in the half, Coach Brown told Allen to reenter the game.

Allen reportedly said, "about bleeping time." Coach Brown sat him back down.

At halftime Allen, who had suffered a right thigh contusion in an earlier game, said he was injured and could not play anymore.

"He said he was hurt, so he didn't play," Coach Brown said. "That's the bottom line. I expected to start him the second half. He said he was hurt."

Allen did not make the trip for the Sixers' next game in Toronto, and speculation began that he was sitting out to spite Coach Brown. Naturally, Allen fired back at critics who dared to question his willingness to play.

"My desire to play?" Allen said. "They're out of their minds. I can't even worry about people who would think (he'd sit out because he was mad at Coach Brown).

"They probably don't know a thing about basketball. For them to say something like that is outrageous."

Eventually, this fight, like many others, died down, and Allen and the Sixers made a push for their first playoff spot since 1991. Allen returned to lineup and scored 27 in a victory over Milwaukee. He also publicly apologized to Coach Brown for swearing at him during the Cleveland game.

With four games left in the season, the Sixers were 26-20, and Allen was playing like an MVP candidate.

"I was asked if I'd rather guard Allen or go to the dentist," Cleveland Cavaliers guard Bob Sura commented. "I said I'd rather go to the dentist. At least there, 20,000 people don't watch that kind of pain."

Through his first 200 games as a Sixer, Allen had averaged 23.5 points, 6.4 assists, 4.2 rebounds, and 2.17 steals. But now the Sixers were in the playoff hunt, and Allen was enjoying the sweet taste of winning.

"As we've gotten closer to going to the playoffs, Allen's first appearance, I've seen him have more focus, concentrate more on winning," Sixers center Matt Geiger said. "His desire has increased, and he doesn't know half of it, because he's never been there."

On May 1, Allen scored 31 points with 9 assists and 5 rebounds as the Sixers beat the Toronto Raptors 103–96 in front of a sell-out home crowd of 20,550 to clinch their first playoff berth since the 1990–91 season.

"I can't find the words to describe how good this feels," Allen said.

In the final game of the regular season Allen scored 33 points to finish the season with a 26.7 point scoring average. That was good enough to finish ahead of Los Angeles Lakers center Shaquille O'Neal (26.3 ppg) and make Allen the Sixers' first NBA scoring champion since Wilt Chamberlain in the 1965–66 season.

Allen also became the sixth Sixer and first since Charles Barkley in 1990–91 to be named to the All-NBA First Team. That honor was particularly satisfying to him because he was voted to the team by the media members with whom he had so often clashed.

"It does feel good to know people recognized me for something positive," Allen said. "It made me feel like I came a long way to be able to get something accomplished like this."

The Sixers (28-22) were seeded sixth in the Eastern Conference Playoffs and underdogs against the third-seeded Orlando Magic (33-17).

Not surprisingly, Allen was nervous about his playoff debut, but once the ball tipped off in the Orlando O-Rena, he was spectacular. Allen had 30 points, 7 assists, and 5 rebounds as the Sixers stunned the Magic 104–90.

"Butterflies?" Allen said. "I might have had a buzzard in my stomach. It was crazy. I felt like once they threw the ball up, everything would be all right, like a regular-season game. Once you run down the court, get banged a couple of times, you're right there where you need to be."

The Magic took Game 2, but Allen had 33 points and 10 steals in Game 3 as the Sixers won 97–85. He then scored 37 with 9 assists and 2 steals as the Sixers clinched the best-of-five series in four games with a 101–91 victory.

The Sixers then went up against the Indiana Pacers, Coach Brown's former team, in the Eastern Conference semifinals. Allen and the Sixers were game, but the veteran Pacers were too much and posted a four-game sweep.

"We accomplished a lot, going to the playoffs for the first time in eight years," Allen said. "It was exciting to come this far. We brought a lot of excitement back to Philly.

"We felt we could've won this series. We have to learn a lot more to be competitive on this level."

The playoffs provided an additional benefit for Allen. With NBC and Turner Network Television broadcasting the games nationally, it was the first time Allen received mass TV exposure to NBA fans. In games and in interviews the nation saw Allen as he was, not as how people told them he was.

Instead of the selfish, disrespectful, egotistical basketball thug, fans across the country got a firsthand look at the hardworking, captivating, dynamic, highly competitive, entertaining young star that Sixer fans had grown to love.

Yes, Allen wore cornrows and flashy jewelry and hip-hop clothes. And yes, he had controversial friends. But fans got to see that he was much more than simply the poster child for DeGeneration X.

15 | Winning Changes Everything

By the end of his third season the national perception of Allen Iverson had started to change. People who had been once quick to criticize were now looking a bit closer.

They saw that there was a lot more substance to Allen than they originally thought. Without question, the exposure Allen got while playing in the playoffs for the first time played a huge role in that.

Suddenly he was not as dangerous or unwelcome as before. Suddenly he was a player to be embraced.

"I thought Allen did an amazing job," Sixers coach Larry Brown said of Allen's handling of his first time in the NBA spotlight. "You always wonder how guys will handle their first playoff experience.

"The games are more meaningful, the pressure's greater, the attention's greater. I loved (Allen's) comments publicly. I liked the way he conducted himself on the court. I loved the way he competed."

It wasn't just that Allen averaged 28.5 points and had 39

assists in eight playoff games. He was terrific in dealing with the media. Win or lose, he showed up for all interview sessions. He had been gracious in victory and reflective in defeat. He had been humble, insightful, funny, and always engaging.

He had been a star, and people like to watch stars.

When the television schedule for the 1999–2000 season was announced, the Philadelphia 76ers were slated for nineteen appearances, eleven times on NBC and eight combined on TNT and TBS.

The eleven NBC appearances by the Sixers, who only had one during the previous season, were the same number as the NBA champion San Antonio Spurs, the runner-up New York Knicks, and the "Showtime" Los Angeles Lakers.

"Last season was so wide open that there were chances for many young, exciting teams to step into the spotlight," said Dick Ebersol, the chairman of NBC Sports. "Interest in the 76ers and Allen Iverson grew as the year went on."

Back in 1997, when the 1997–98 season guide was released by the NBA, Minnesota Timberwolves guard Stephon Marbury, not Allen, who was the Rookie of the Year, was pictured on the page highlighting outstanding rookies from the previous season. Clearly, the NBA was sending a message to Allen, who had been arrested on misdemeanor drug possession charges during the summer of 1997.

But when the 1999–2000 Official NBA Register came out, Allen had joined Julius Erving and Moses Malone as the only 76ers to grace the cover of the book.

"We're seeing Allen taking a center position in the marketing of the league," Sixers Senior Vice President Dave Coskey said at the time. "This is unbelievably cool."

Allen was excited, but still realistic about what was happening.

"I hate to say this, but winning changes things," Allen said of his newfound popularity with the media. "I'm still mostly the same person. People are just starting to accept me now.

"Now people are starting to see another side of me, that I have a family that I care about, including two children who I'm at home taking care of."

But Allen had also started taking control of things around him. He said his children, Tiaura and Allen II, had "matured me, made me want to make better and smarter decisions, so I can set a good example for them."

His friends, who had become the subject of so much debate his first two seasons, were still around but had taken a much lower profile.

"My friends and I have been through a lot of things in our lives," Allen said in a poignant commentary on HBO's *The Chris Rock Show.* "We've messed up just like everybody else.

"But all of us are getting better. We've been poor for twenty-plus years, and I finally came into some money and I do want to live a little bit.

"I know my friends can make things hard for me if they mess up. I've been embarrassed by some of the things that have happened. I don't want them to happen again, and my friends know that.

"They understand that if they get in some trouble and they're affiliated with me, it's going to come down on me.

Still, the best thing that I can say about myself is that I've remained true to my inner-city roots."

Which is why, despite being named First-Team All-NBA and being one of the most popular players in the league, Allen was not doing hot-dog and underwear commercials like more clean-cut stars like Kobe Bryant and Grant Hill.

Madison Avenue was still leery of the kid with baggy jeans, cornrows, and tattoos. But that was okay with Allen. While he wouldn't have minded having the marketing appeal of a Michael Jordan, he did not want that if it meant sacrificing his individuality or integrity to himself.

"If I want to see myself on TV, I can just turn on ESPN every night," Allen said. "I'm not big on having a bunch of commercials and all that. That's not what it's all about. If they're going to market me, I want to be the way I am."

And the way Allen is:

Cornrows—"I'm not going to change my hair."

Baggy shirts and pants—"All these people want me to wear Italian suits all the time like Michael Jordan. I don't like to wear suits."

Jewelry—"We love being flashy, having flashy jewelry. When I was little, my mom and I used to sit in the dark and talk about jewelry, all the cool jewelry we were gonna have some day."

Hip-hop—"We all dress hip-hop. We love hip-hop. I mean, that's our generation right now."

And of course, Allen Iverson is tattoos, although when he first entered the NBA, the only one he had was the one on his left arm—a bulldog with his nickname "The Answer" above it.

Since then Allen has added:

EAST END, for where he grew up, the east side of New-port News; CT, the initials of a friend who died; a panther; BAD NEWS; the Chinese symbols for belief and loyalty; his children's names, TIAURA and DEUCE, on his right chest; CRU THIK, his recording company; the Tibetan symbol for strength; praying hands with his mother's and grandmother's initials above them near his heart; HOLD MY OWN; VA's FINEST; DYNASTY RAIDER; his rap-per's identity JEWELZ; ONLY THE STRONG SURVIVE; a skull wearing a soldier's helmet; and of course, the words FEAR NO ONE around a screaming ghoul with its arms on its head.

In 1999 the NBA was embarrassed and apologized to Allen when the cover of *Hoop* magazine featured a photo of him with his tattoos airbrushed out.

"That was an insult," Allen said. "I wish they wouldn't use me at all if they can't accept all of me. I have things on my body that are just tattoos to others but mean a lot to me, about my mother, my grandmother, my kids, my fiancée. These aren't just tattoos to me."

16 || Raising the Bar

This newfound success meant raised expectations for the Sixers, and the 1999–2000 season was being looked at as one of great promise.

Not only was the team coming off its first playoff appearance since 1991, but Allen had led the league in scoring and had made the All-NBA First Team.

"We're not going to sneak up on anybody this year," Coach Brown said as the Sixers opened training camp in Chapel Hill, North Carolina. "We've got to bring our A game every night, which is the fun part of making the next step."

Allen was ready. He had his first taste of the playoffs, liked it, and wanted more—much more.

"I've had too much time off," Allen said. "I'm ready. My expectations are high. If I didn't think (we could win a championship), it would be unfair to my teammates, to the coaching staff, to the fans, myself, my family, my kids. If I didn't believe that, then I'm doing it all for nothing."

By the start of the 1999–2000 season, Allen was the only player left from the team that Coach Brown had taken over in 1997.

Without Allen, the team looked like a collection of role players and lunch-pail workers. But that was the beauty of it. Coach Brown had surrounded Allen with a group of hard-nosed, unselfish grinders who didn't care about anything but winning.

This, in turn, allowed Allen to be Allen without the stress of jealousy over shots or attention.

"They really built a team around Allen," Allen's first professional coach, Johnny Davis, would say later. "They took all of his strengths and they surrounded him with players who could complement his many talents. If you're not playing against the Sixers on a particular night, it's a beautiful thing to watch because it's great basketball."

Still there were issues to be worked out, particularly between Allen and his good friend Larry Hughes, the second-year guard from St. Louis University.

The Sixers drafted Hughes with the idea that he could log big minutes at both the point and off guard, but veteran Eric Snow had played well at the point the year before and Allen was thriving as a two guard.

Coach Brown wanted to find minutes for the high-flying twenty-year-old, but Hughes's ballhandling and decision-making were not solid enough for him to play the point. In effect, he had basically become the backup to the best scorer in the league.

"I have no preference," Hughes said at the start of training camp. "I came in as a two guard, even though I played some point in college. But I'd really like to be off the ball where I can slash to the basket and get to the offensive boards."

Coach Brown had said that Allen should expect to play 14 to 18 minutes a game at the point, but he wasn't confident things would work smoothly.

"Allen's not going to change the way he plays," Coach Brown said. "He can get stronger as he gets older, but he won't ever change his style. I wouldn't want to see him change. But he's going to have to get everybody involved, be a quarterback, not be the first, second, and third option himself."

Once again this was a situation waiting to boil over.

Allen seemed excited as the season approached, but a day before the opener at the NBA Champion San Antonio Spurs, he made a strange comment.

"Lately, it hasn't been fun for me," he said. "For whatever reason, a personal reason, the game hasn't been fun since training camp. It's basketball in general. It's not fun right now. I want to get the love back. I always said I'd play basketball regardless of whether they paid me or not. If I was broke right now, I'd still be in some park, probably playing ball.

"It won't come with winning. When I was a rookie, we were getting our butts kicked, and I still had a great time. It won't have anything to do with winning. It's me, I started feeling a different way.

"Once the season starts rolling, once we start playing games, maybe all of this will change. I'll handle it myself. I don't think it will take a lot to start loving the game. If I can't find the love, I don't think there's any need for me to play."

Whatever Allen's malaise was, it affected the whole team as the Sixers started the season with three straight losses.

Allen put the responsibility on himself.

"Me, my game," said Allen, who had made just 19 of 57 shots. "I look at these games we've lost, and if I played the game I'm capable of playing, we don't lose. It's as simple as that."

Allen bounced back in the home opener with 37 points as the Sixers beat Seattle 117–98. In addition, Larry Hughes scored 27 starting for Eric Snow.

Had the Sixers' backcourt of the future finally arrived? Not by a long shot.

During the next game in Orlando, Allen scored 46 as the Sixers beat the Magic 110–105. Larry Hughes played just 17 minutes.

"I can't check myself in," Hughes said. "If it's meant for me to know why I didn't play more, I'll be told."

But that controversy was nothing compared to the one that came after the game.

Coach Brown had met with Sixers veterans Eric Snow, George Lynch, and Aaron McKie a couple of weeks earlier and suggested they establish some dress standards—suits or sport jackets on road trips.

Those players agreed, but no one had asked Allen.

"It might be a mistake on my part, it might be something I don't like, but I never dressed like that in my life," Allen said.

"Before last season's playoffs, I never wore a suit in my life. People see me like they know me."

"We say the Lord's Prayer as a team. If somebody doesn't believe it, don't say it," was Allen's response when asked if he was going to abide by the team's newly instituted dress code.

In truth, the designer hip-hop gear Allen wore probably cost as much as an Italian suit.

"This is no dramatic thing," Coach Brown said of the dress code. "We did it in the playoffs. I just wanted to make things clear-cut. My thing is, people saw Michael Jordan and Scottie Pippen when Chicago was winning those championships, and they remembered how they looked. It made an impression. We've got a lot of games on national television. I want people to see us in suits."

Not surprisingly, they weren't going to see Allen in one.

"There might be a little beef about it, but if they take my money, so be it," Allen said, noting that he would pay a fine before wearing a suit. "It's not going to matter. I'm going to wear what I want to wear."

The dress code didn't stand, but in a game against the San Antonio Spurs, Allen broke the thumb on his shooting hand and was lost for three weeks. The amazing thing was he had broken the thumb in the first half but still finished the game, scoring 35.

"This isn't the right time for this to happen," Allen said. "I need to be playing. I can't do my team any good sitting on the sideline."

The Sixers went on a three-game winning streak without Allen, but in early December the first trade rumors concerning Larry Hughes surfaced.

But even when he wasn't playing, Allen could find trouble, even if of a minor sort. On December 9, long-time Sixer Charles Barkley, now a member of the Houston Rockets, was playing his last game in Philadelphia, but Allen called in sick for the game.

A local sports-talk radio station, however, reported that Allen was seen having dinner at his favorite eating establishment instead of being in bed sick. Many callers said Allen was just spiting Barkley, who had been critical of him in the past.

Allen said he was indeed sick but went out because he got hungry.

"I'm sorry the whole thing happened," said Allen. "If I had known it was going to have this type of response, I would have never have come out. I would have eaten a peanut-butter-and-jelly sandwich."

The Sixers went 6-5 with Allen out of the lineup. He returned on December 11 and scored 11 points on 5-of-16 shooting in a blowout loss to the Charlotte Hornets. But in the next game he hit 37 points in a victory over Toronto.

Things seemed to be falling back into place, so of course, it was time for another blowup between Allen and Coach Brown. But this one would be the worst ever.

The Sixers were playing in Detroit and had lost by 23 points to the Pistons. Frustrated with the play of his starters, Coach Brown benched them for most of the second half, including Allen, who sat for the final 20 minutes and 15 seconds.

Allen was furious, and he let everyone know it. He felt Coach Brown had embarrassed him.

"For some reason, my style doesn't fit this team anymore," Allen told reporters after the game. "If that's the way it is, something needs to happen. Something's got to give. If I'm hurting this team, I need to get out of here.

"I don't like what's going on. When I get back to Philly, I'll let that be known. However you look at it, I'm going to be the bad guy, but I'll deal with it. I've never been done like that in my career."

Allen did not attend an optional practice the next day. Coach Brown wasn't conciliatory in his remarks, either.

"I sat down all the starters, not just one," Coach Brown said. "My door is always open. If a guy needs to talk to me, they know where to find me. If it was such a pressing and urgent matter, I was pretty accessible, and I'll always be accessible.

"I learned a long time ago that sometimes you're not very objective after games. Anybody who watched that game understood something needed to be done. That's what I did. That's not going to change. We start guys for a reason.

"I don't want to trade anybody, but I'm going to do what's best for the team."

What Sixers president Pat Croce decided was that Allen and Coach Brown should get together with him and General Manager Billy King for a closed-door airing out.

"My role in this is to get them in a room together," Croce said. "I believe in communication. They have to meet, work this thing out.

"It made me nauseous when I saw the word *trade*. I don't want Allen wanting to be traded. I don't want dirty laundry aired in public. It ruins the harmony of the family. I don't want ultimatums from anyone. It's no good. How can the word *trade* come from out of the air?"

A couple of days later Croce had his meeting with King, Coach Brown, and Allen before the Sixers' home rematch with the Pistons.

Brown was not happy at being forced to meet with Allen. He felt it undermined his authority and later said it was the only time he had ever been upset with Pat Croce.

Whatever was said during the ninety-minute sit-down, which both sides said got loud at times, it worked. The Sixers beat the Pistons in overtime 122–121 on a buzzer-beater by Eric Snow.

"Believe me, this is the perfect ending to this day," Allen said. "I could sit here and tell you everything in that meeting was great, but I would be lying. I'm not going to say everything was peaches and cream.

"But I can say that after I left out of that room, I felt good about Coach Brown; I felt good about myself and I felt good about this organization. It was the most real talk I've had with Coach Brown."

Later it was reported that Coach Brown had told Allen immediately after the incident in Detroit that "I don't know if we can go on like this. If we don't fix this situation, I'm going to have to resign."

Team sources said Allen talked Coach Brown out of quitting, saying, "We're in this together. Neither of us are going anywhere."

Neither Allen nor Coach Brown was under the illusion that they would no longer have flare-ups, but both agreed they had to figure out a better way of dealing with them.

"I think the one thing I found out through this is that I've got to figure out a way that I can support the kid," Coach Brown said. "I have to find out a way to point out when he does something that's not in our best interest or his best interest in a way that he can handle it."

In mid-December, the twelve-man roster for the 2000 United States Men's Olympic basketball team was announced. Many people believed Allen deserved a spot, and he had been in consideration. But he was not named to the team.

"It's not something God is ready for me to do right now, that's the only way I look at it," Allen said of not being selected. "I'm from Newport News, Virginia. When I look back at guys from Newport News, I don't see any in the NBA. I don't see anybody who has achieved the things I have.

"When I'm not invited to play with another team, it wasn't meant to be. I'm not on that team, but I know I get to play another team, get to wear an NBA uniform."

The Olympics weren't in Allen's immediate future, but his first All-Star Game was. Allen was the leading vote-getter among guards in the Eastern Conference and third-leading vote-getter overall.

He would be a starter in the 2000 All-Star Game in Oakland, California.

"That's the fans," Allen said proudly. "Fans don't care about the other stuff. They care about who is best at that position. Without them, it still might've been hard to get on the team."

In the regular season the Sixers were 14-14 on Christmas Day. Allen was averaging 29.4 points, but the team still had the third worst offense in the league. They were headed on a five-day, four-game West Coast swing that could make or break their season. In the games Allen totaled 97 points as the Sixers ran off wins against Seattle, Golden State, and Vancouver.

Later in January Allen would match his career-high of 50 points while taking an incredible 40 shots in a 119–108 victory over Sacramento.

At the All-Star Break, the Sixers record was 27-23.

Allen made his All-Star debut, and led the East with 26 points and 9 assists. Had the East not lost 137–126, Allen probably would've won the MVP Award.

Allen wowed his fellow All-Stars.

"I consider myself a true fan," Dallas Mavericks guard Michael Finley said. "I know who can play. Guys who can do as many things as Allen does are the prototype of the future."

"Oh, man, if I were to play with Allen, all he'd have to do is get open," Phoenix Suns point guard Jason Kidd said, "and he has no problem doing that. This is a guy who can score 50. It would be easy to play with him."

"Why wouldn't you want to play with Allen?" Miami Heat center Alonzo Mourning said. "I hear people say he shoots too much, but if he's making them, I say, 'Shoot, Allen.' "

"It was just a great experience for me," Allen said.

With thirty-two games left in the regular season, the Sixers were ready to make a playoff push. But there was a lingering issue that needed to be resolved.

*   *   *

Larry Hughes did not want to be a point guard, and he certainly was not going to replace Allen as the shooting guard. And as the February 24 trading deadline approached, a move seemed inevitable.

"I don't like the fact that my teammates go into games night after night not knowing if they're going to be here," Allen said during the All-Star Break. "Some guys can't play with their names out there like that.

"I want Larry to stay, but that goes beyond basketball. He's my friend. It would be crazy for me to say I want him to leave."

Inevitably, the trade did come. In a three-way deal Hughes was shipped to the Golden State Warriors, and Toni Kukoc, who had helped the Chicago Bulls and Michael Jordan win three NBA titles, landed in Philadelphia.

For a team desperate for a second-scoring option to Allen, Kukoc seemed like the perfect fit.

"This helps the team a lot," Allen said. "I don't think they could have made a better deal. It'll be hard for people to double-team me now. That's what I'm looking forward to. (Kukoc) adds so much to the team, not just scoring, but his overall game."

The Sixer were 34-26 and just two and a half games behind the Atlantic Division leading Miami Heat when they went to South Florida for a showdown.

And then Allen slipped up again.

Allen missed the morning shootaround, saying he had a headache. He called Sixers trainer Len Currier to say he was staying in his hotel room, but Coach Brown, with the backing of Pat Croce and Billy King, suspended Allen for the game against the Heat, which the Sixers lost 92–77.

Allen, who lost $109,756 in salary, was angry.

"I feel like I've been here four years, they know who I am as a player and a competitor," said Allen, who admitted he had been out late on the town in Miami. "You think I'm going to come to Miami and not go out? I go out if I want to.

"But don't question my heart. Don't question my health. I don't think this was fair at all. I'm not going to bite my tongue on this at all. If I get sick and we have another shootaround, I'll do it the same way and deal with the repercussions."

This time, though, the repercussions went further than Coach Brown.

At the Sixers home game against the Utah Jazz, Allen was booed by a good portion of the sell-out crowd of 20,705, many who came to get bean bag dolls of Allen called "Alien Iverson."

By the end of the game, however, he had everyone cheering as he scored 24 points with 9 assists and 3 steals as the Sixers upset the Jazz 99–97.

"That's the way life is," Allen said of the mixed fan reaction. "You can't satisfy everybody. There are going to be a billion fans who love Allen Iverson, a billion who hate me. Once you start worrying about the ones who hate you, that's when you lose focus."

Coach Brown, for one, did not want Allen to get booed.

"I think the boos were the worst thing that could happen, so it had to be hard for Allen," he said. "We did something (in Miami). We hope there's closure. Whether we agree or not, it's done and it's over. The saddest thing is, a lot of things are handled internally, but this was real public because he got suspended. I told Allen it has to be over or it damages everybody."

The rest of the season was relatively quiet. Allen had suffered several injuries during the season, and played the last few weeks of the season on a broken big toe on his left foot. Coach Brown got a contract extension, meaning that he and Allen were going to be together for the next five years.

"We might clash again, we might not," Allen said. "Our conversations are like two brothers, or a father and son. We can argue. We can get into it, and when it's over, we still love each other."

The Sixers finished the regular season 49-33, were seeded fifth, and faced the Charlotte Hornets in the first round of the Eastern Conference Playoffs. Allen scored 40 in Game 1 as the Sixers won in Charlotte, but the bigger news was his angry postgame outburst at General Manager Billy King. In an interview in *The Charlotte Observer*, King had made a comment that Allen interpreted as questioning whether or not the relationship between him and the Sixers could work long-term.

"If I hear my general manager say he doesn't know if the marriage is going to work to some reporter, it's time for him to stop feeling that way," Allen said. "I was shocked to hear Billy's comments. I was hurt. Don't get me wrong. I never want to leave here. I love Philadelphia, but for people to say that I'm the franchise player, that's ludicrous. I'm not treated like a franchise player. I'm treated like the twelfth guy on the bench."

King apologized because, while he didn't believe he said what Allen thought he said, he didn't intend to hurt Allen's feelings.

On the court Allen cracked a bone in his ankle in a Game 2 loss. He kept playing as the Sixers beat the Hornets in four games, but point guard Eric Snow was severely hobbled by a chip fracture in his right ankle that had caused him to miss Games 3 and 4.

That was bad news because next up for the Sixers was the Indiana Pacers, the team that had swept them out of the playoffs the year before.

But the top-seeded Pacers had their eyes on their first NBA Finals appearance. They beat the Sixers 108–91 in Game 1 and 103–97 in Game 2.

After the Pacers went up 3–0 with a 97–89 victory at the First Union Center, they added insult to injury by writing "And now . . . they sleep. R.I.P." on the chalkboard inside their locker room.

The Sixers rebounded to win Games 4 and 5, but Indiana ended the Sixers' championship dreams for the second straight season with a 106–90 victory in Game 6.

"They taught us something tonight," Allen said while fighting back tears. "We aren't closer to them because we still lost the series. I don't care that we won two games. I wanted to win four and go on to the next round.

"I love the heart we showed, but I've seen that all year. I'm aware of that. I, myself, have to get better. We have to get better as a team. We have a long way to go."

During the turbulent summer of 2000, Allen almost ended up going further than he ever expected or wanted.

17 | A Summer of Discord

Once again, Coach Larry Brown was frustrated.

The Sixers' 49 victories in the 1999–2000 season was the franchise's most in a decade, and they had reached the Eastern Conference semifinals for the second consecutive season. Allen, who had averaged a career-high 28.4 points, was a first-time All-Star and a second-team All-NBA selection.

But the team was clearly flawed.

"We are just not good enough to win a championship right now," Coach Brown surmised the day after the Sixers were eliminated from the playoffs. "I'd love to tell you differently, but that's just the bottom line.

"We were just exposed in some areas, and it was very obvious. The goal is to improve every single year, to get closer to accomplishing our goal of a championship. We can't honestly say that if we do nothing to change this team."

In the days that followed, it would soon become apparent that Coach Brown was not only frustrated—he was also angry.

In addition to the public incidents, word was out that Allen had missed or been late for numerous other practices and shootarounds.

Allen's name was again being mentioned in trade rumors.

"It's very rare one of the marquee players' names gets mentioned, especially a young kid," Coach Brown said. "But there are a lot of things over the years that (Allen) has done that maybe people think you might get tired of.

"If we think a trade benefits our club, I don't think anybody is untradable. I don't want to break up the core of this team, but we have to investigate every opportunity."

Allen was home in Hampton, but he knew his name was out there. During the NBA Finals between the Los Angeles Lakers and Indiana Pacers, he made a call to Lakers Hall of Famer Earvin "Magic" Johnson seeking advice.

"He said 'You've been there. You've done it,' " Magic said of the call. "I told him that it's simple. He has to be more a part of the team. He needs to sit down with (Coach Brown). Sit down with (Pat Croce).

"The star has to set the example for everybody. And I think now he's starting to understand that going to practice, getting there on time, getting paid the highest salary, that's what goes along with being a star. That's the responsibility. When I was playing, I was the first one to practice and the last one to leave."

But it appeared that this time, it might be too late to save the marriage.

If there had been a power struggle between Allen and Coach Brown, then it was clear that the coach had won when he signed a contract extension toward the end of the season.

On the night the Sixers drafted Hofstra University point guard Craig "Speedy" Claxton, Coach Brown said, "Maybe Allen's got to learn to share some time with other people. He obviously can't play forty-eight minutes a game the way we want him to play."

Philadelphia was split. It seemed just as many fans sided with Allen as Coach Brown.

The rumors continued. One had Allen being offered to the Detroit Pistons for Grant Hill. Another had him being offered to the Los Angeles Clippers for rookie swingman Lamar Odom.

In July, Coach Brown was given permission to talk to the University of North Carolina, his alma mater, about its vacant head coaching position.

At the same time Allen was hosting his annual charity benefit weekend in Hampton. He aired his feelings publicly for the first time.

"It'd be extremely hard," Allen said of playing for Coach Brown again. "It'd be crazy to think that everything would be peaches and cream, because it's not. I didn't play this year for my coach. I played for the fans of Philadelphia, for myself, and for my teammates.

"I did play for (Coach Brown), too, and I want to be part of any success we have, but I just went through too much. It's going to hard to just swallow that.

"For me to say I would be happy with that, everybody in Philly would know I'd be lying or just saying whatever needed to be said to make sure this doesn't get out of hand.

He's the coach, and I just have to roll with that. I just want to be in Philly regardless."

Allen had also made a promise to the Sixers that he was going to do something special the next season whether Coach Brown was there or not.

"Something better than I've been doing, a lot better than what I've been doing," he said. "I'm going to dedicate myself to get ready to do what I've planned. If Coach Brown is there, I have no problem. I'm coming to play basketball."

Having taken his name out of consideration for North Carolina, Coach Brown was going to be back with the Sixers. Whether Allen would also be back was less clear.

Coach Brown seemed to be becoming more combative in his tone every time he spoke.

"I don't think Iverson's an issue with me at all if he comes on time, if he wants to practice, to practice on a daily basis," he said. "If he wants to follow the rules all the other players follow, then he's not going to have a problem with me at all.

"But if it continues to be a situation where he's late, he doesn't practice, he doesn't do the things the other players do, then it's going to be a problem.

"I've been hearing the same conversations about 'I'm going to change and I'm going to do better' for four years. Somewhere along the line, you've got to say 'Hey, I've got to be responsible enough and care about the team enough.' I don't know what the answer is, but I'm tired of everybody talking about my relationship with Allen Iverson.

"If his rhetoric again is right about how he's going to do things right, then he'll be here and be a big part of this team. But I remember the end of the (1998–99) season, we talked about the things he needed to do, and it didn't change. I had a great conversation (with Allen) after this season, so we'll see. I'm hopeful, but . . ."

It was clear for now that Coach Brown didn't believe Allen, or at least, not enough to take another chance with him.

Pat Croce called Allen, who again said that he would change. Croce believed Allen, but he also knew that guaranteeing that Coach Brown would not trade him was not something he could do. As vice president of Basketball Operations, Coach Brown also had final say in all basketball-related decisions.

As usual, Croce was straight-up honest with Allen.

"Everything was going down with the trade talk," Croce recalled of that summer. "I called Allen out of respect for him, and I said look, I can't defend you this time. The things you're doing, Bubba-Chuck, I can't defend you," he said, using Allen's nickname.

" 'You're going to get traded.' That's when he went off. Allen said, 'Pat, I'll change. I can do the things (Coach Brown) wants.' I believed him, but it wasn't up to me."

Late in July word was out that Sixers General Manager Billy King had engineered a massive four-team trade between the Sixers, Detroit Pistons, Los Angeles Lakers, and Charlotte Hornets.

Allen and Sixers center Matt Geiger would end up in Detroit, while the Sixers would end up with Charlotte free agent All-Star guard Eddie Jones, Los Angeles Lakers forward Glen Rice, and Detroit forward Jerome Williams.

The deal had been all but done, but Matt Geiger refused to relinquish a $5 million trade bonus that was in his contract with the Sixers. For salary cap purposes, this made the deal unworkable for the Pistons.

"We did trade Allen," Coach Brown would say later in the season when asked about the proposed trade.

Instead, on August 3, Eddie Jones forced Charlotte to trade him to the Miami Heat. Jones was the player the Sixers had wanted most in the trade; without him, they did not feel they could get fair value back in moving Allen.

This was as about as ugly a situation as anyone could imagine.

Allen had been traded to Detroit, and he knew it. Yet suddenly he was back with the people who he surely felt had betrayed his loyalty.

Knowing that Allen would likely come back to Philadelphia angry, the Sixers tried to calm things by backing away from the talk that now Allen had to be traded no matter what.

"It's almost like people say everything wrong in the organization is because of Allen; it's not," King said. "Everything that has gone on isn't Allen Iverson's fault. He did help us win a lot of ballgames. I can't say he destroyed everything around him.

"If I wanted to trade Allen, I could do it today. Would I get value? No. If you trade a player like Allen, you've got to get a great player back. You can't give him away."

Late in August the Sixers re-signed Toni Kukoc to a four-year contract. Allen was officially off the trading block. King had talked to Allen, and it didn't sound as if Allen would be coming to training camp angry. In fact, Allen had told King just the opposite.

"Allen expressed to Billy that nobody ever criticized the way he played," Coach Brown said. "It's just been a matter of being on time, being conscientious about respecting his teammates, and respecting the game.

"He said to Billy those are things he can control, and he expects to change. I don't know why he would say to Billy that he was prepared to do all that and not do it. I am looking forward to talking to Allen, and I'm hopeful this'll be the end of that saga."

Allen, for his part, had said he was going to do "a lot better than what I've been doing."

The 2000–2001 NBA season would be the first of the new millennium.

Allen Iverson said he was going to be a better player and a better man. No one could've known just how incredibly his prediction would come true.

18 | The Answer Delivers

Considering the way the 2000–2001 season started, it would hard to believe that it would turn into such a memorable one for Allen, the Philadelphia 76ers, and the entire basketball community.

No sooner had the Sixers opened training camp at Penn State University than controversy was yet again swirling around Allen.

While Coach Brown was with the United States Olympic team preparing for the 2000 Olympics in Sydney, Australia, Allen had spent much of the summer in the recording studio, delving in his other passion—hard-core rap music.

As his rap alter ego, Jewelz, Allen had recorded his first album tentatively titled *Non-Fiction*. Following the gangsta-rap genre that made artists like Tupac, Dr. Dre, and Eminem platinum-selling artists, Jewelz's lyrics were raw. His first single, "40 Bars," featured expletive-laced language that spoke of gun violence and was degrading to women and offensive to homosexuals.

"I know the chances I'm taking," Allen told *The Philadelphia Inquirer* in an article that ran the day before the Sixers' Media Day. "The media are going to tear my (butt) up, just like they've been doing since I got into the league.

"(The album) is about life, period. I still deal with every aspect of it; the sex, the violence, the drugs, all that. It's never going to go nowhere. And if it does start to fade away, I still won't forget it. I know where I come from. I know what I've been through.

"I still got anger. I'm going to let it out on wax. I'm not trying to provoke nobody or go out and hurt nobody or anything. It's just hip-hop."

Despite his staunch defense of what he'd done, a lot of people, not just the media, went after him hard. Calls into sports talk shows were comparing him to Atlanta Braves relief pitcher John Rocker, who had been suspended from baseball for making offensive comments about minorities and gays.

On Media Day, Allen was assailed with questions about "40 Bars." He said he was there to talk about basketball, not music, so the questions turned to his allegedly missing up to fifty practices the previous season.

"Yeah, I was late to practice," Allen said, "but I'm not even brave enough to miss that many practices."

Allen wasn't getting any support from his Sixers' family about "40 Bars." This was his issue alone to deal with.

"This is an Allen Iverson issue; he has to defend his statements," Sixers President Pat Croce said. "It's not a 76er issue. He's the only one who can defend or describe what he meant in the lyrics."

Allen issued a written apology saying in part that "if individuals of the gay community and women of the world are offended by any of the material in my upcoming album, let the record show that I wish to extend a profound apology."

There were questions about whether the Sixers or the NBA would suspend Allen, but both declined, saying that while they found the lyrics offensive, it was not their policy to suspend a player for exercising his First Amendment rights.

Commissioner Stern, however, also said that offended fans could be expected to verbally express their displeasure with Allen.

The song "40 Bars" got some radio play, but the album—later retitled *Misunderstood*—twice had its release postponed.

"It's just an art form," Allen said. "People hear about a gun, and they think I'm talking about killing somebody. A lot of people don't understand that when rappers talk about a gun, we're talking lyrically, rapid fire, our mouth is our weapon."

Surprisingly, the flap over the rap album did not last long, and once the season started, Allen and the Sixers, who were now considered one of the favorites in the Eastern Conference, were all about basketball.

From the beginning, Allen was a noticeably changed player, more focused on the complete game, not just scoring. Allen wasn't shooting particularly well, but he was doing all of the other things to help the Sixers jump out to a franchise-record 10-0 start.

"He's all about playing the right way," Coach Brown

said. "If you examine it, he's just playing ball. His defense is 100 percent better, his turnovers are down, he's getting rid of the ball sooner and enjoying it more. I hear a couple of jerks in the stands yelling for him to shoot. But the one thing I had always hoped, once he won the scoring title and made the All-Star Game, was that he'd start to realize all of that is great but that the bottom line is about winning.

"You can't convince a player until he buys into the program. He's more comfortable with the players around him. His overall game is the best since I've been here."

Allen was doing all of the things he said he would do. He had asked to be a team captain again, and Coach Brown said he could with the condition that he live up to the responsibilities of it.

"It really does start with me," Allen said, echoing the advice that Magic Johnson had given him. "I set an example on and off the court, being the first to come, the last one to leave. My teammates see that, and they feed off that.

"When I first came into the league, everybody saw the talent and they wanted to make me a guy who was thirty-five years old. Nobody ever gave me room to make a mistake. I'm just getting better, learning how to win."

The Sixers were rolling at 14-4, but disaster struck when point guard Eric Snow went down with a stress fracture in his right ankle. Fortunately, sixth-man Aaron McKie, Allen's best friend on the team, moved into the starting spot and was a success, and the team kept rolling.

Then the Sixers lost 112–94 at home to the Dallas Mavericks. Despite their 17-5 record, Coach Brown went on a tirade, but this time several players shouted back at him, saying that he was pushing too hard, and they were giving their all.

Allen said Coach Brown was treating them as if they were losing.

The next game against the Bulls in Chicago, Coach Brown barely spoke to his players, and then when they resturned home, he missed two days of practice.

Rumors began to float that Coach Brown had tried to quit but was talked out of it by Pat Croce and Billy King. Eventually, Coach Brown returned, saying that he just needed a break from himself, his team, and basketball.

"A lot of stuff in the (team meeting) is family business," he said. "Reading some of the reports, there are things that weren't really factual.

"I feel good. I needed the break. I'm okay. I've given guys personal days off before on this team, and it hadn't been an issue. It's an issue when a coach does it?"

Not with the players.

"I think everybody is making this out to be a little more than what it is," Allen said. "Coach had personal issues to handle. Everybody is trying to dig between the lines for me when it's just that."

Still the Sixers lost their next two games, and Allen suffered a dislocated right shoulder in a collision with New York Knicks guard Chris Childs. He was expected to be out three weeks. Instead, Allen missed five days and one game. He returned against the Golden State Warriors, scoring 29 in a victory.

"I knew I was going to play," said Allen, who followed up

with a 46-point effort at Sacramento. "I felt like I wasn't going to hurt myself any more than I already was."

The Sixers finished the calendar year at 21-8.

Allen started the New Year by scoring 21 against Atlanta, 41 against Seattle, and a career-high 54 against Cleveland to win NBA Player of the Week honors for the second time.

It was the start of an incredible January during which he averaged 34.6 points, 4.4 assists, and 2.67 steals. The Sixers went 13-3 and Allen was named NBA Player of the Month.

"It's definitely something I'm going to cherish for the rest of my life," Allen said.

The Sixers were 41-13 with one game remaining before the All-Star Break. Allen was again voted in as a starter. Coach Brown was going to direct the Eastern Conference squad, and Sixers center Theo Ratliff was also going to start.

But in that last game against the Houston Rockets, Ratliff suffered a stress fracture in his right wrist and would be lost for at least six weeks. With backup center Matt Geiger having already missed most of the season with a leg injury, the Sixers were down to second-year centers Todd MacCulloch and Nazr Mohammed.

With twenty-eight games remaining, Coach Brown and general manager Billy King had to decide if that would be enough at center to carry the Sixers through.

The 2001 All-Star Game was held in Washington, D.C., where Allen had played collegiately at Georgetown University.

It turned into a landmark weekend for him.

On the Saturday before the game, Allen was invited to appear on the NBC TV show *Meet the Press*, with host Tim

Russert, the Washington bureau chief of NBC News, on a show on sports and how it crossed over into real life.

Allen appeared with Russert, NBA commissioner David Stern, and Los Angeles Lakers star Shaquille O'Neal.

"I never expected anything like this when I first came in the league five years ago," Allen said of the opportunity to talk to the nation on a respected news show. "I was so honored just to do it. But I want people to hear me, not judge me on what they've heard or read.

"I think it's important for people to understand that we're human, too. We do make mistakes just like everybody else. It's just concentrating on being a better player, a better person, better father, better husband, for me."

Among other things, the panel discussed the responsibilities of players and fans, the role-model issue, vulgarity, and racism. Russert, who was used to interviewing politicians and heads of states, was impressed with Allen.

"I watched Allen at Georgetown, I watched him as a young player, struggling with himself," Russert said. "Now I see someone with more discipline, extraordinarily gifted, saying things that are so important for kids to hear.

"For Allen Iverson to say on *Meet the Press* that you have to be responsible, there are fifteen- and sixteen-year-old kids who might not listen to me say that, but to have that come from Shaq, from Allen, those are pretty good choices. If even one or two kids out there make a change in their lives, that's good. It's important to let people see sports heroes, to hear them talk about their own experiences in a very direct way."

The All-Star Game that followed was Allen's moment. He scored 25 points, including 10 of his team's final 16 as the Eastern Conference defeated the Western Conference 111–110.

And to cap it all, Allen was named Most Valuable Player.

"The best feeling is to win, to be the MVP in front of my mom, my friends, Coach Thompson, the people in D.C., who have been fighting for me from day one. I don't have words to describe how I feel," Allen said.

The Sixers went 5-0 after the All-Star Break to improve to 41-14, the best record in the league. But management was still concerned about not having a big-time presence in the middle.

On the night of the NBA trade deadline, the Sixers rolled the dice and made a blockbuster deal.

Coach Brown traded Ratliff, reserve forward Toni Kukoc, Nazr Mohammed, and reserve guard Juan Sanchez to the Atlanta Hawks for All-Star center Dikembe Mutombo.

"I think the final moment was when we realized we were going to be without Theo for sixteen, twenty games, or who knows when," Coach Brown said. "We're hoping to position ourselves in the playoffs and give ourselves a chance to win a championship. We figured that with Dikembe, we would have that opportunity."

Mutombo is a 7-1, 280-pound shot-blocking wizard. He was a three-time NBA Defensive Player of the Year and the league's leading rebounder. Also, like Allen, he had played his college ball at Georgetown University.

Allen and his teammates were unhappy about losing Ratliff, who had been to wars with them for three years, but he was realistic about the business of trying to win a title.

He knew that Mutombo made the Sixers formidable.

"I'd be lying to all of you if I said (Mutombo) couldn't help us win a championship," Allen said. "He's a rebounder. He's an intimidator. He can change the game by himself from the center position."

Because of various injuries, Allen missed nine of the final twenty-seven games. That hurt the Sixers' chemistry in trying to get used to Mutombo. The team closed out 15-13, which was well below their previous pace, but their fifty-six victories were the most in the Eastern Conference. The Sixers won the Atlantic Division for the first time since the 1989–90 season.

With a 31.1 point scoring average, Allen won his second scoring title and became the first player since Michael Jordan to average more than 30 points for a season.

He was one of the favorites to be named NBA Most Valuable Player.

Still, this entire season was all geared toward achieving success in the playoffs. And the Sixers' first opponent would be their nemesis—the Indiana Pacers.

"A championship, that's what I'm expecting," Allen said as he prepared for his third playoff run. "Nothing less. I know people might think it's crazy for me to say that because we haven't been out of the second round the last two years.

"But just knowing my teammates, knowing what they expect out of this season, knowing how hard they worked, along with myself and the coaching staff, we can't settle for nothing less."

19 | A Run to Glory

The 2000–2001 NBA Playoffs began with the Sixers feeling supremely confident.

Their 56-26 record was the best in the Eastern Conference, and they would have home-court advantage all the way to the NBA Finals.

The Indiana Pacers were hardly the same team that had gone to the NBA Finals the previous year. Head coach Larry Bird had been replaced by Isiah Thomas and several key players had retired or been traded. But All-Star Reggie Miller and Jalen Rose were still with the Pacers, and these two had been the primary culprits in eliminating the Sixers the previous two years.

The Sixers also entered the playoffs hurt. Point guard Eric Snow had come back early from a fractured right ankle and was playing at about 75 percent health. Allen and guard Aaron McKie were bruised and battered. Forward George Lynch was the only player who had made it through all eighty-two games.

"We're the better team this time," Snow proclaimed before the series started. "We just have to take care of business."

The Sixers were in control of Game 1, leading by as much as 18 late in the third quarter. But their attack went stale, and the Pacers fought back to within two points with less than six seconds remaining.

Pacers guard Reggie Miller drained a three-pointer with two seconds left to stun the Sixers and the sold-out crowd at the First Union Center 79–78.

"I thought we got to a point where we thought, 'We've got these guys beat,' " Allen said. "Our (butts) got tight. It's as simple as that."

Despite facing demons of the previous two seasons, the Sixers did not panic.

Allen scored 45 to outduel Reggie Miller, who poured in 41 points, as the Sixers ran away with Game 2, 116–98.

Coach Brown would call it the best game Allen had ever played because he managed to deal with the double-team defense the Pacers threw at him, to not only score but also hand out 9 assists.

"I'm going to remember this game for a long time," Allen said. "I have been doing a lot just off of my God-given ability, but this game took a lot of thinking."

In Game 3, Miller scored a game-high 35, but Allen dropped 32 points and 6 assists, while Aaron McKie added 22 points as the Sixers won 92–87.

In Game 4 at Conesco Fieldhouse in Indianapolis, Allen scored 33 as the Sixers held off the Pacers 88–85 to win the opening-round series 3–1.

"I told Allen afterward that he has to make his team believe they can win," a gracious Reggie Miller said. "We put them through enough wars. This is their first step."

Allen was as emotional as ever, crying tears of happiness as he walked off the court.

"This is so special," he said. "We could never get by this team. Those were tears of joy. I know it's only the first round. I'm not acting like we won a championship, but for a team that has beaten you two years in a row, shattered your dreams, it feels good to beat them."

Next up for the Sixers were the Toronto Raptors. The best-of-seven series would be a marquee matchup of two of the NBA's brightest young stars—Allen and Raptors' star Vince Carter.

The series was dubbed "The Answer versus Vinsanity."

Allen scored a game-high 36, but Carter scored 35 and Dell Curry added 20 points as the Raptors beat the Sixers 96–93 in Game 1.

With the Sixers desperately needing a win, Allen amazed everyone in Game 2 by sinking 21 of 39 shots and setting a franchise playoff record with 54 points. He scored 19 of the Sixers' final 20 points in a 97–92 victory.

"How many guys are you going to see come into a playoff game and just dominate at six feet tall, just doing whatever he wants on the floor?" Sixers guard Aaron McKie asked. "It was a beautiful thing."

In the next game Carter set a NBA record by making nine consecutive three-pointers. He had 50 points to lead the Raptors to a crushing 102–78 victory in Game 3.

Then, once again, it was Allen's turn. His 30 points in Game 4 helped even the series at 2–2.

Game 5 was in Philadelphia, but the day before it was announced that Allen had been voted the 2000–01 NBA Most Valuable Player. He had joined immortals Wilt Chamberlain, Julius Erving, and Moses Malone as the only Sixers to be named MVP.

By totaling 1,121 points and receiving 93 of 124 possible first-place votes in voting by sportswriters and broadcasters, Allen winning the MVP became a testament to how much he'd grown in his five NBA seasons.

"With everything that went on during the summer, the only thing I thought about coming into this season was winning the NBA championship," Allen said. "I felt that for me to turn everything around, I had to push myself to win a championship.

"I didn't start with the other guys. I started with myself first. I always told (Sixers guard Aaron McKie) that it was going to be important for me to become a professional, like he is day in and day out.

"I just tried to look in the mirror and work on the things I wasn't doing right as a person and a ballplayer. I made a promise to myself that after the season I would look in the same mirror and be able to say that I did everything I could."

Coach Brown also had a moment of realization during Allen's award ceremony.

"I'm really proud to have had the opportunity to coach Allen, and I never thought I'd say that," Coach Brown said. "I'm so proud of what Allen has done.

"Maybe I didn't give it enough thought or time to understand what this kid's about, and that's the neatest thing about my improved relationship with him.

"He doesn't always do it the way I would expect or sometimes like. But I know where his heart is. This kid has great character, and he cares about people that he trusts and knows have his best interests at heart.

"You guys know how this marriage has been. But I couldn't have scripted it any better to see how he has grown as a person. Forget the basketball, we all knew he has great talent. He's just developed so much as a human being and a teammate. I can't imagine any player having a better year or a bigger impact on a team or a city."

Game 5 was going to be tough for the Toronto Raptors. Allen was given his MVP trophy in front of a sell-out crowd, and the Raptors were always up against it. Allen scored a game-high 52 and said afterward, "The basket looked like an ocean."

But they weren't done yet. The Raptors won Game 6 to tie the series 3–3 and set up a decisive Game 7 in Philadelphia.

By this time, the personal scoring duel between Allen Iverson and Raptors star Vince Carter had taken on classic proportions. The Answer and Air Canada had both averaged close to 40 points in the series, and another high-scoring showdown was expected.

But Allen had a different idea. The Raptors double-teamed him to limit his lethal scoring touch. So Allen changed his game—he decided to be a point guard again.

Aaron McKie led the Sixers with 22 points, but Allen, who

scored 21, had a career-high 16 assists. Still, it took Vince Carter missing at the buzzer for the Sixers to advance to the Eastern Conference Finals with an 88–87 victory.

"I just wanted to do something special," said Allen, who suffered hip and butt injury. "Anything to help my team. The way you draw it up if you're a scorer is that you have a great scoring night to help your team. In a million years I didn't believe that I would come out and have a career-high in assists."

In the Eastern Conference Finals, the Sixers finally started a series right by beating the Milwaukee Bucks, 93–85, behind 34 points from Allen.

But All-Star guard Ray Allen hit for 38 points in Game 2 to even the series.

The injury Allen suffered in Game 7 against Toronto wasn't getting better. He'd had been hurt before. He'd even missed games because of injuries. But this was different.

This was Game 3 of the Eastern Conference Finals and the Philadelphia 76ers and Milwaukee Bucks were tied at 1–1 with the next two games scheduled to be played in Milwaukee's Bradley Center.

Allen had injured his tailbone in Game 7 against the Toronto Raptors when he collided with Charles Oakley and fell hard to the floor. He had played through the pain through the first two games but had not been as effective as he wanted.

"If I play like this," Allen said after the Game 2 loss in which he scored just 16 and missed 21 of 26 shots, "if it's hurting my team, I might have to sit out. It's just something you have to think about.

"This is my dream. To get hurt this bad right now? I've been hurt all season long with different kinds of injuries. But I never had to play with an injury like this one."

Coach Brown decided to sit him out of Game 3, and the Sixers lost 89–83.

Allen was back for Game 4. Early on he took an elbow from Ray Allen, which bloodied his mouth. Had the officials seen him bleeding, Allen would have had to leave the game.

Once again Allen showed his toughness and willingness to do anything to win. When his mouth filled up with blood, Allen swallowed it, rather than let it be seen.

He scored 11 of the Sixers' final 13 points in an 89–83 victory.

Eric Snow would be the hero of Game 5. Still healing from a fracture in his ankle, Snow suffered another break in the same ankle but played on. He scored 18 and made the game-winning shot in an 89–88 victory.

Allen had suffered through a 5-for-27 shooting night and scored a playoff low 15 points. But he was more than satisfied.

"In the past if I went 5-for-27, I don't think we'd win," Allen said. "But now, I feel so good about it because I really feel we are a team. For me to struggle like that, and we still put it together and got the win. We don't care how we win, whether it's pretty or not."

The Sixers were one victory from their first trip to the NBA Finals since winning the championship in 1983, but the Bucks blew them out 110–100 behind 41 points from Ray Allen. Despite the loss, Allen, who had struggled with his shooting throughout the series, erupted for 26 points in the fourth quarter to finish with 46.

Now it was Game 7 of the 2001 Eastern Conference Finals. At stake for both the Sixers and the Bucks was a spot in the NBA Finals.

Allen had played the entire Bucks series with a severely bruised tailbone. After each game, he hobbled off the court like a man three times older than his twenty-five years. The injury forced him to sit out Game 3 and had caused him to shoot poorly through the first six games. Still this was Game 7, and the Sixers needed a bruised Iverson to give them whatever he could, or their season was going to be over.

He did not disappoint. Allen poured in 44 points with 7 assists, 6 rebounds, and 2 steals. Dikembe Mutombo, who before the game had rashly guaranteed a victory, had 23 points, 19 rebounds, and 7 blocked shots as the Sixers dismantled the Bucks 108–91 to earn a date with the Los Angeles Lakers in the NBA Finals.

"I just approached the game knowing that I had to do something on the court, just help, just contribute," said Allen. "I didn't have to score 40 points or get a triple-double or have 10 assists or anything like that. Just do something, maybe just something in the last seconds to help my team win.

"I just wanted to set a good example," Allen said. "I wanted to do the things that I hadn't done before. My whole thing was to just try to be professional. I think when you work hard, good things happen, obviously so, because we're going to the Finals."

20 | Just a Little Short

During the regular season, the Sixers had finished with the same 56-26 record as the Los Angeles Lakers, and they had split their regular season meetings with them. Despite these stats, however, virtually nobody gave them a chance against the defending NBA champions. The Lakers had smashed through the Western Conference playoffs, sweeping the Portland Trail Blazers, Sacramento Kings, and San Antonio Spurs.

The Sixers were being called the biggest underdogs in Finals history.

"The Lakers should be confident," Allen said. "If I went through the playoffs, and we had not lost a game, I would think we weren't going to lose at all. They are supposed to feel that way.

"But there's a flip side to that. We didn't make this long trip just to come out here, roll over, and die. We're going to play every one of these games like it's our last because we don't know that we'll ever get this opportunity again."

As ever the NBA Finals were a media circus. More than a thousand journalists from around the world were there. Lakers stars Shaquille O'Neal and Kobe Bryant were big stars, but without question the player most in demand was Allen Iverson.

His story was one of the most compelling ever in the Finals.

Despite his tattoos and cornrows and hip-hop image, Allen had become the new face of the NBA. His #3 jersey was the top-seller for the NBA.

"I see a human being in the process of growing, who wants to be the consummate basketball player, a team player, a good family man," NBA commissioner David Stern said. "It's amazing, as you do get older, you do get wiser.

"He's doing great."

Still, the media kept pushing the angle of the "new Allen Iverson." Tiring of it, Allen decided to set the record straight.

"I don't care," Allen said when asked about the public's changing views of him. "All I care about is what my family feel about me, my friends, my teammates, the people who always cared about me.

"Nothing easy about life. Nothing easy about winning a championship. Nothing easy about being Allen Iverson where everybody is looking at your every move, criticizing you for just saying a curse word when you get mad. Making you feel like you're some type of villain, the smallest man on the court but the biggest villain in life.

"No way, I'm never going to put my guard down."

As Game 1 of the finals approached, the Sixers weren't about to let the doubters shake their confidence.

"Let everyone talk all they want," said center Dikembe Mutombo, who had the daunting task of defending Shaquille O'Neal. "I know the talkers will do their job, but we're the ones who will play basketball. Someone who knows basketball knows anything can happen on the court."

And "anything" did happen in Game 1.

Showing no signs of being intimidated in their first championship game, the Sixers stunned the Staples Center crowd by jumping out to a 73–58 lead, but the Lakers scored 19 of the final 25 points and trailed just 79–77 going into the fourth quarter.

In the end, Allen and Shaquille O'Neal both had 41 points in regulation as the teams went to overtime tied at 94. The Lakers scored the first five points in the overtime, but the Sixers rallied. With 1:19 on the clock, Allen drained a three-pointer to put them up 101–99. He then scored with 48.2 seconds left.

Allen had seven points in overtime as the Sixers stunned the Lakers with a 107–101 overtime victory.

Afterward, he had a message to deliver.

"Big-time underdogs," Allen said with a smile. "Everyone saying we can't do it gives us extra drive. People coming in here with brooms gives us extra drive.

"There are so many so-called basketball experts. The only people who know are the ones on the floor. I'm glad nobody bet their life on (a sweep), because they'd be dead. We've got heart. We're going to play with that first, talent second."

The Sixers' celebration was short-lived as it was revealed that Aaron McKie had suffered a chip-fracture during the game. That meant the Sixers would go into Game 2 with two guards—McKie and Eric Snow—playing on fractured ankles.

The Sixers kept fighting in the Finals, but the injuries and fatigue were too much to overcome.

Shaquille O'Neal, who was named NBA Finals MVP for the second consecutive year, was devastating. In Game 2, Shaq had 28 points and 20 rebounds as the Lakers won 98–89.

In Game 3, Robert Horry hit a clutch three-pointer as the Lakers held off the Sixers 96–91.

O'Neal was back in Game 4 with 34 points and 14 rebounds as Los Angeles took a commanding 3–1 lead. Game 5 was more of the same as Shaq scored 29 points with 13 rebounds. The Lakers won 108–96 to close out the Finals, 4–1, and claim their second straight championship.

"After that last game was over, I couldn't really concentrate on losing, knowing that the season was over," Allen would later say. "All I could say was 'Now I get a chance to heal.' Everything else hit me later on.

"I just felt good about what we accomplished, what the city accomplished, everything we had been through. It was a great season, one that helped me out in my basketball career. Now I have what it takes to get to that point.

"All I can think about is getting better. This season is going to help us. And Coach Brown knows he can lead a team to the Finals.

"We drew a nice picture. We just didn't finish it."

The Finals had provided another opportunity for the world to see Allen Iverson for who he was, and to find out again that he wasn't so bad.

"It's a good thing because people try to understand me instead of just judging me from the mistakes I made in the past, and the way I look, who I'm around," said Allen, who turned twenty-six during the Finals. "You know, I think people need to take the time to pay attention to who I am. I'm still the same person. I'm just older, wiser. I still make mistakes. I just learn from them and get better.

"The Sixers were talking about getting rid of me. I heard a lot of negative things, even from some fans. I just kept working. Eventually they accepted me for who I was inside, not my hair, my jewelry, who I hang with, my music.

"When I was growing up, everybody laughed at me when I said I was going to be a professional basketball or football player. All those guys are in jail or dead or still at home. I'm not laughing at them, but I'm laughing now.

"I did it my way. I never changed who I was. I'm still the same person, just smarter, older, more mature. I feel good about who I am."

Visit
❖ **Pocket Books** ❖
online at

....

www.SimonSays.com

....

Keep up on the latest new
releases from your favorite
authors, as well as author
appearances, news, chats,
special offers and more.

SIMON & SCHUSTER
A VIACOM COMPANY
www.SimonSays.com

Pocket
Books

2381-01